LIVING IN
PORTUGAL

LIVING IN PORTUGAL

THE ESSENTIAL GUIDE FOR PROPERTY PURCHASERS AND RESIDENTS

Susan Thackeray

ROBERT HALE · LONDON

© Susan Thackeray 1985

First published in Great Britain 1985
Reprinted 1987
2nd edition, 1988

Robert Hale Limited
Clerkenwell House
Clerkenwell Green
London EC1R OHT

British Library Cataloguing in Publication Data
Thackeray, Susan
   Living in Portugal: the essential guide
   for property purchasers and residents.
   —2nd ed.
   1. Portugal—Handbooks, manuals, etc.
   I. Title
   914.69'0444   DP517

   ISBN 0-7090-3243-9

Set in Linotron Sabon by
Rowland Phototypesetting Limited
Bury St Edmunds, Suffolk
Printed in Great Britain by
St Edmundsbury Press Limited
Bury St Edmunds, Suffolk
Bound by WBC Bookbinders Limited

Contents

domicile and protecting your assets. Pensions. Legal
and health precautions. Disposing of unwanted
belongings. Books and other ex-pat problems. A
driving licence in a hurry?

For Michael and Simon,
with love

Acknowledgements

My thanks to Sr Miguel Arouca, Pro-Consul at the British Embassy in Lisbon and to Donald Armstrong MBE, Vice-Consul in Portimão for their help. Also to António Correia of the Portuguese National Tourist Office, Lisbon, Julie Baring of Luz Bay Club, Pauline Berry, Paddy and Anita Gaston, Gauntlett International Transportes Lda, Carlos Alberto Gomes, Erik Holben of United in Almansil, Gloria de Melo Kanzis of TAP Air Portugal, John and Dinah Kelly, Maria Carolina de Jesús Correia Marquês, Marvila Lda of Lagos, John and Madge Measures of the West Algarve Riding Centre, Vitor Manuel Martins Milhano, John and Jenny Murat, Tom and Helen Pidd, Colin and Trudy Purser, Maria Terésa França Bento dos Reis, David Sherwood of Autoborne Lda, Dr Jorge Silva, Dra Maria Alice Pestana Serrano e Silva, Walter and Britta Stamy, Bill and Marge Start of the "53" in Lagos, Dave Wade, Tim and Sheila Wales . . . and especially to the wonderfully well-informed and most generous of Collective People, Patricia Walker Bijou:

Obrigada

Preface

Although this book is concerned with mainland Portugal as a whole, it is only fair to point out that our own Portuguese living has been done exclusively in the Algarve. Which many Lisboans will tell you is not the same thing at all.

It is, of course. Admittedly life is rather slower here in the south, the attitude to time even more cavalier. And the Algarve does seem to have its own peculiar way of doing things. Nevertheless, the Lisbon-made laws that interest foreign residents—the ones about property, importing cars, documentation, taxation, driving and so on—are as valid here as they are anywhere else in the country.

But those laws can change at alarming speed. Even before Portugal became a member of the European Economic Community on 1 January 1986, there was a torrent of legislation from the Assembleia da República as the country battled its way out of an economic crisis and embarked on its own development programme. Now there is even more legislation, largely to do with Portugal's gradual integration into the EEC, but also on the domestic front. In this last year there have been any number of changes affecting the man-in-the-street and the woman-in-the-supermarket, whether they are foreign residents, prospective residents or Portuguese nationals. And there will undoubtedly be many more changes by the time you read this.

Please, therefore, do not take anything for granted. Check carefully with as many knowledgeable people as you can find before buying Portuguese property, importing your belongings or starting to collect up your various Portuguese documents.

Most of the prices given here were valid in 1986, when there were 210 escudos to the pound. These, I'm afraid, will almost certainly increase.

S.T.
Algarve

List of Illustrations

Picture credits:
Photographs are reproduced by courtesy of the Portuguese National
Tourist Office: 1, 3–4, 6–8, 11, 13–15, 17–21; Michael Carreck: 2,
10; and Paul C. Waldock: 5, 9, 12, 16, 22–24.

Recommended Reading

The Selective Traveller in Portugal, Ann Bridge and Susan
Lowndes (Chatto & Windus, London)

Pousadas of Portugal, Sam and Jane Ballard (Ballard's Travel
Guides, PO Box 647, Gig Harbor, Washington 98335,
USA—and perhaps now available in Britain)

Portugal—The Impossible Revolution, Phil Mailer
(Solidarity (London), 123 Lathom Road, London E6)

A New History of Portugal, H. V. Livermore (Cambridge
University Press)

Algarve, David Wright and Patrick Swift (Hutchinson
Publishing Group Ltd., London)

They Went to Portugal, Rose Macaulay (Jonathan Cape,
London)

The Rough Guide to Portugal, Mark Ellingham and John
Fisher (Routledge & Kegan Paul plc., London)

Sintra and Its Farm Manors, Arturo D. Pereira, Felipa Esprito
Santo Cardoso and Fernando Calado Correia (published
in four languages at Estalagem Quinta dos Lobos, 2710
Sintra, Portugal)

Portuguese Wine, Raymond Postgate (J. M. Dent & Sons
Ltd., London)

1. Escape from the Snow

"Moving out of the province, are you? I can't say that I blame you. So many people seem to be leaving Montreal these days."

The lady who had just made a very acceptable offer for our aged stereo produced a fat wallet and began counting out notes. "Where are you going, if you don't mind my asking—Toronto?"

"Portugal."

She was astounded. And so, to a lesser degree, were we.

Not astounded that we were finally packed and poised to leave Canada after more than twenty years, but still a bit surprised to think that we were moving east. For the last ten of those twenty years we had been very busy trying to move ourselves south.

Back in the mid-60s we had decided that the wickedly cold Montreal winters were not for us. As soon as we were free of school bills, mortgage payments and other monetary millstones, we would escape both the climate and the city rat-race. Not to mention the increasingly tedious political upheavals that were gathering strength and which, by that spring of 1978, had already driven thousands of French- and English-speaking citizens over the provincial border into Ontario and all points west.

We knew exactly what we were looking for, and it obviously lay to the south. A place where the sun shone every day and flowers bloomed all year round. Where the living was simple and two donkeys constituted a traffic jam. Where snow was only ever seen on Christmas cards, and ice in long, cool drinks. And where, with luck, we might even be able to pick breakfast oranges off our own tree.

It was, of course, a fairly common daydream. But we were more fortunate than many of our friends who cursed the winter and longed for a place in the sun. Because so much of our work was connected with travel, we were able to visit many of the places that looked promising on paper, and our Escape Routes file was fat with information about Cat Island, Eleuthera, Cayman Brac, the Turks and Caicos, Belize, San Andres, Anguilla, Providencia and a collection of other primitive, low-profile spots—including, heaven help us in retrospect, El Salvador.

Europe was out of the question. Too cold. Except perhaps for the Mediterranean area, which did not appeal to us greatly. Besides, we had already hauled ourselves and our belongings across the Atlantic once, when we had emigrated from Britain in 1957, and once was quite enough.

We might still be sitting in the snow gazing steadfastly southwards and making hopeful little forays to undeveloped dots on the map, if it had not been for the Portuguese national airline. Out of the blue, Transportes Aéroes Portugueses, as they were called in those days, asked my husband if he would care to visit and then write about the southern part of Portugal.

In June 1973, after a stop-over in Lisbon, he had stepped onto the sizzling tarmac of eight-year-old Faro airport and into the blazing Algarve sun.

Lisbon, he said later, was the loveliest city he had ever seen. Clean, colourful, elegant and beautifully mannered; a city where you could stroll at night and never even think about being mugged. Where you could linger for hours over a cup of coffee, watching the passing scene, without so much as a small sigh of impatience from a waiter. It had ancient buildings, some of them elaborately decorated and faced with hand-painted tiles. Great green parks and steep cobbled roads, British-style pillar-boxes of that special British red and double-decker buses.

It was ridiculously inexpensive, too, by Canadian standards. I forget now what his bill was for a sumptuous night with breakfast at the prestigious Ritz Hotel, but I do remember that we had paid as much—if not more—for a very indifferent motel room in Canada.

In a week and a rented Mini, he had wandered from the eastern Algarve border town of Vila Real de Santo António

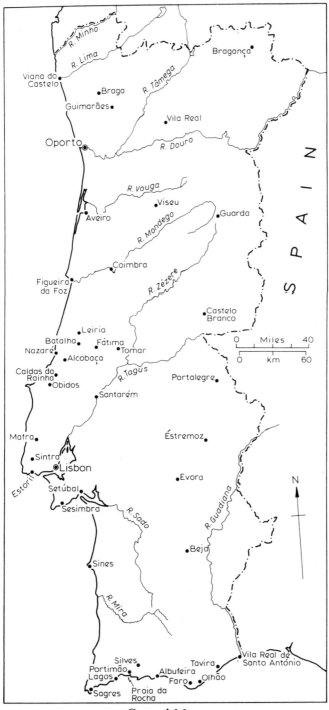

General Map

down to Cape St Vincent, the most south-westerly point of
Europe. He could have done the journey quite easily in a single
day, had he wanted; Portugal's southern coastline is hardly a
hundred miles long. But since he was being paid to explore, he
took his time and followed every signpost off the main
east-west road, to wander through each town, village and
collection of small whitewashed houses.

It was, he reported, like being in two different countries in
two different centuries.

Along the coast, the sun-tanned tourists shared huge sandy
beaches with fishing boats and squid pots, while net-mending
fishermen sat a polite distance away and goggled at the bikinis.
Scantily dressed families patronized sidewalk cafés, reading
yesterday's *Daily Mirror* or watching the very properly
collared-and-tied Portuguese go in no great hurry about their
business. There were as many donkey-carts as cars in the
neatly swept towns, and pedestrians paid no heed to any of
them. They and their dogs ambled slowly across the streets,
looking neither left nor right, confident they would not be
mown down.

In the pleasant coastal hotels a spotless room and a Continental breakfast cost not much more than three Canadian
hamburgers, and with the highest standards of service. Tiny
pageboys, with buttons gleaming and pillbox hats set perkily
askew, struggled with suitcases and whistled up taxis for
departing guests. In the restaurants, white-jacketed waiters
who looked hardly old enough to conjugate *Amare* could fillet
a freshly caught sole and peel an orange with the dexterity of a
West End waiter twice their age.

Flowers grew everywhere. Cascading over walls, clambering up lamp-posts and palm trees in the municipal gardens,
flourishing riotously along the roadsides. Every cottage window had its box of brilliant geraniums, and it seemed as
though anyone who came across a patch of unadorned earth
anywhere in a town felt obliged to plant something colourful
in it.

A mile or two inland and away from the gentle bustle of the
tourist coast, a couple of centuries slipped away and the
scenery changed dramatically.

Here among the fig trees and orange groves, small farms sat beside sun-browned fields, white-washed single-storey buildings with terracotta roofs and flowerpots brightening up the walls. Scraggy chickens and small black pigs foraged amiably together. Goats, *café-au-lait* North African-looking sheep and sleek brown oxen grazed on the hillsides, or in the shade of eucalyptus and mimosa trees. Mules and well-tended donkeys pulled carts together or plodded monotonously in circles to work the rusty water-wheels which looked as though they had been there since the Middle Ages. They had, we discovered later. Introduced by the Arabs during the Moorish occupation of Portugal, along with the rice fields and the fruit farms, the *noras* that still provide many Algarve farms with water are essentially the same as they were more than a thousand years ago.

Even in 1973 there was scarcely a television aerial on the horizon, few motor-bikes and even fewer cars along the country roads. Most of the small rural cottages were lit by oil lamps, and the women did their family wash in the streams that meandered through the fields, draping gorse and cistus bushes with linen drying in the scorching sun. It was hot and dry and Biblical, back there in the foothills among the dusty almonds and olive trees, and it seemed in keeping to pass a long-skirted, barefoot woman striding along with a water jug or a bundle on her head. Or a shepherd sprawled under a fig tree with his dog sprawled beside him, while his sheep safely grazed on the sparse greenery.

"I think we might have found our escape route," Michael said when he got home. "Why don't you go as soon as you can, and see if you'd like to live in Portugal?"

What with one thing and another, five months went by before I was able to make a swift detour to the south of Portugal on my way back from a visit to Britain. I left on a bleak and beastly November day when Heathrow's runways were ankle-deep in rainwater and the snow that crowned the Pyrenees reminded me that it was time to put up the storm windows in the Montreal house.

But if the travel brochures were to be believed—and I had written enough of those to be just a little cynical—the Algarve ought to be bathed in sunshine.

It was. And warm sunshine at that, late in the mid-November afternoon.

Faro's cafés were still crowded. Elderly Portuguese ladies stumped along the shady side of the street, shielding wrinkled faces with huge black umbrellas. Jovial British, Dutch and German tourists promenaded in shorts and sun-dresses, and I could not wait to shed my layers of sweaters.

From the hotel window I looked down on a neat public garden of flowering hibiscus, jasmine, carnations, trumpet vine and lilies among the still-naked jacaranda trees and leafy palms. Assorted dogs dozed in shop doorways, while customers picked their way carefully over and around them. Beyond the gardens and the leisurely honkless traffic, fat seagulls and brightly painted rowboats bobbed gently in the small walled harbour.

I felt instantly and happily at home.

The area that had appealed most to my husband lay about sixty miles west of Faro. Its centre was a beautiful historic town that had seen Carthaginians, Romans, Visigoths and Moorish invaders come and go, and had welcomed Nelson's sailors exuberantly whenever the British Fleet anchored in its enormous bay.

On the last of the three days I spent in and around this most attractive town, I was introduced to the tiny fishing community that became our home. It was hardly even a village in those days, just a huddle of cottages, some white, some pastel coloured, around a bayful of boats and as untidy as anything you are ever likely to see in Portugal.

Some of the small houses may have had electricity and running water, but the majority of cottagers appeared to use paraffin lamps and the village tap. The drainage system was mostly do-it-yourself: buckets were emptied casually into one of the two steep cobbled roadways so their contents could dribble gently down the hill and into the sea. Chickens roamed freely, dodging dogs and donkey carts. And in the village square that first afternoon, several hundredweight of black, loudly protesting pig was being chivvied into a cart, while a small crowd gathered to give advice.

The friendly estate agent who had brought me to the village, and who had not quite grasped the fact that we had no money to buy houses (possibly because I had not made that as clear as I might have done) showed me a converted cottage with small, cramped rooms and a spectacular view over the bay. He quoted a price in pounds, which, when I had got myself into Canadian dollars, seemed inordinately large. But the untidy little village was a gem, drains and all, and I longed to live there.

I flew merrily home.

The price of the cottage, we agreed, would have been laughable even if we had had any money. However, we were in no great hurry. Unless something quite unforeseen happened, there were seven more miserably cold Montreal winters to be survived, which gave us plenty of time to explore and consider. Michael would make the next trip to Portugal, probably in the spring, and see how he felt about this unlikely Utopia of a village.

On 25 April 1974—just ten days before he was booked to fly to Faro—we woke to find lovely, low-profile Portugal all over the news. The Carnation Revolution was under way, tanks were rumbling through the streets, the political police had shot several people, and it looked as though our Portuguese dream was over before it had even begun.

We decided to wait and see what happened.

Post-Revolution Lisbon looked rather different when Michael finally got there, twenty-one months behind schedule. The city was dishevelled, with painted slogans and torn posters on the ancient walls, rubbish littering the once-pristine streets. Prices had soared and, instead of well-heeled tourists, refugee families from the newly independent African colonies now filled the four- and five-star hotels, at the Portuguese government's expense. The days were enlivened by demonstrations, and people marching sternly about with clenched fists; the nights by loud-hailer vans bellowing political messages through the city.

The hotel barman was gloomy. "No nice girls in Lisboa now," he said to Michael, his sole customer. "Only prossi-tooties."

In the southern province and to an outsider's eye, the aftermath of revolution seemed less drastic. The streets were untidier than before, and there were plenty of scrawled slogans —including one about independence for the Algarve. Building was at a standstill, many large houses stood forlornly empty, and there was a noticeable dearth of foreign tourists. But there was no feeling of tension that a stranger could discern, and the smiles were as warm as they had been before.

In our favourite town, the beautiful hotel had more staff than guests, and the service was overwhelming. There were notices, though, stuck up in the reception area, warning about impending strikes. The pageboys and the twelve-year-old waiters had all vanished—back to school, presumably, where they belonged.

The friendly estate agents were still in business. Just. And overjoyed to see someone who was even remotely interested in Portuguese property. One of the partners whisked Michael off to see the over-priced cottage in the small untidy village. When he said no, he didn't think so, thanks very much, he was promptly shown architect's drawings for a planned apartment block on the other side of the bay. For the same price and providing we could wait a few months, we could have the top-floor flat-with-a-view and a great deal more space. Furthermore, we could pay for it over four years, if we liked. The flat, said the agent with his hand on his heart, would be ready for us to move into within nine months.

Possibly. It was an attractive idea, but we wouldn't be ready to move out of Montreal within nine months. Especially now that we were on the verge of committing ourselves to earning extra money to pay for a Portuguese apartment.

We discussed the interim rental prospects. In spite of appearances, the village had been extremely popular with pre-Revolution tourists from Britain, and they had filled every rentable corner from mid-May until the end of September. Not, obviously, for the last two years, 1974 and 1975. Revolutions, however bloodless and carnationy, do tend to discourage visitors and, as far as the outside world knew, things had not yet got back to normal in Portugal. There would not be much in the way of tourism in 1976, either, or even in 1977.

But by 1978 the Algarve would surely be back in its principal business of providing holidays for sun-seekers. We could, we learned, contract what would be a most desirable holiday residence to the local tour company, and do quite nicely out of it until we were ready to shake off the snows of Montreal in, we estimated, the spring of 1980.

It was one of our best-laid plans—and we should have remembered what happens to those.

By the time the flat was finished, only a year and a half later than promised, life and working conditions in Montreal had deteriorated sadly. The new rabidly separatist provincial government was insisting that everyone live, work and be educated in French. Our friends and clients were fleeing like lemmings over the border into English-speaking Canada, and the For Sale signs sprouted like toadstools on Montreal's front lawns.

Should we join the exodus and work out our remaining two years in Toronto or Calgary? Or should we count ourselves political refugees, push off to Portugal before we had planned and hope for the best? We were still dithering when the cable came from the builder. The apartment was now finished, and could he please have the next payment?

We started packing for Portugal.

Now there is an enormous amount of preparation involved in forsaking one home to set up another, even if the move is only across town. To move successfully and without nervous breakdowns from a familiar environment to one that is foreign in every respect, from language and culture down to doubtful drinking water, you probably need to allow at least a year. We did it in four horrible snowbound months, which was ridiculous and not to be recommended. By the time we all landed in Lisbon, we looked and felt like a family of Salvation Army rejects, so fraught that it took far too long to get our collective nerve-ends back where they belonged and to wind ourselves down to the gentle Portuguese way of life.

Our whirlwind departure was the first of many mistakes.

It is not easy to start a new life in a foreign country, no matter how many times you have visited that country or how much you may love it. Emigration is a traumatic experience, as we already knew, and the older you are, the more difficult it is to discard the habits of a lifetime and take on new ones. That was something we had not taken into account. Simple every-day things like cashing a cheque and looking up a telephone number have to be learned all over again. The first circular letter we received from our Portuguese bank frightened us half to death, because without a great deal of effort and a diction-ary we could not tell at a glance if it contained good news or bad.

Some people who emigrate find it hard at first to get used to the idea that they are now the foreigners. And that the way things were done wherever they came from is not the only way.

This is an extremely hospitable country, and foreign resi-dents are not regarded or treated as second-class citizens. But, reasonably enough, the Portuguese prefer to do things their way—and it is useless for foreigners to grumble that the Portuguese system takes time.

You may easily spend the best part of a day waiting to pay your annual dues at the local tax office, and thinking how much easier it would be just to put a cheque in the mail. But that is not the Portuguese way. And if you watch the official behind the counter, you'll see why. He, poor patient soul, spends a large part of his day completing tax forms for elderly people who cannot read or write.

Today's Portugal is quite a bit different from the one we first saw in 1973, and a whole world away from the Portugal that old-time residents remember back in the very early 1960s, when there were few foreigners living outside Lisbon and Oporto and when the Algarve was still virgin territory for tourists. When you come to live here, you will undoubtedly hear plenty of stories about those Good Old Days. When a four-course dinner cost a few bob, wine sold for pennies a litre, and land could be bought for small change. And when Portu-guese fishermen who had not yet learned about supply and demand would gladly give a crab away to anyone who asked for it.

Those far-off days were certainly good for the foreigners, but not necessarily for the poorer Portuguese, many of whom had to send their young children out to work to augment the family income. Those were the days of widespread illiteracy, strict censorship and a secret police force. When it was forbidden to join a union, to strike, to write political slogans on walls or anywhere else, and to sell anything as decadent as *Playboy* magazine.

Though life is still hard for the working Portuguese in 1987—with high inflation, rising prices and a serious unemployment problem—it is a great deal better than it was before the Revolution. The children are being educated, at least up to the age of fourteen, despite a chronic shortage of both schools and teachers in the rural areas. There are social services and a minimum wage, vastly improved communications and medical facilities, and a more up-to-date outlook in high places.

The winds of change that have been blowing through Portugal at gale force must leave some of the old people breathless and bewildered. Their grandchildren are growing up knowing how to read and write not only in Portuguese but also in English and very often in French as well. The girls are out of the kitchen and into the great big world of science and commerce; a nursing career is no longer regarded as the next best thing to prostitution, which was the attitude only a very few years ago. Divorce, unlawful and unheard-of in Dr Salazar's day, is now legal. So is abortion, under certain circumstances.

Even the sun-worshippers have been allowed to come out of their closets; or, more accurately, out of their secluded and illegal coves. Last summer there was television footage from one of the newly designated nudist beaches in the Algarve, which must have shocked elderly Portuguese ladies out of their thick woollen socks. Not so very long ago, when bikinis were in vogue everywhere else in the world, men were forbidden to go topless on Portuguese beaches. If they wanted to swim or lie in the sun, they had to wear one-piece silent-movie-type bathing suits.

There is so much legislation pouring out of the Assembleia da República these days that it is impossible for the average Portuguese citizen to keep pace with it. And a foreigner would not have a hope. Which is why, in the following pages, you will find you are constantly being urged to seek good, reliable and preferably professional Portuguese advice on all matters of importance.

There are dramatic changes, too, in the Portuguese landscape; especially in the Algarve, where building resumed with a vengeance soon after we arrived and has been going on apace ever since.

We have watched donkey tracks turn into paved roads, empty fields into mini-villages and our own grubby village double—if not treble—in size. Now it is quite a respectable summer resort, with reasonable drainage, admirable street lighting, half a dozen new restaurants, telephones all over the place, three swimming pools and some tennis and squash courts. We miss our lovely view over the hills, now blocked out by concrete. But that's progress, I suppose.

One thing has not changed, however. In spite of all their financial and political problems over the last twelve years, the Portuguese remain some of the kindliest, friendliest and most tolerant people you could ever wish to meet. Even the bureaucrats—and there are a great many of those—are helpful and courteous, infinitely patient with dim-witted *estrangeiros*. If you are planning a new career as a foreigner, there is no better place than Portugal.

Our first few years in this country have been immensely happy ones. Which is not to say that we did not occasionally find ourselves in difficulties. If we had known in 1978 what we have gleaned over the years, we could have saved ourselves a great deal of trouble and anxiety—and saved our kindly friends and neighbours the bore of having to bale us out and point us in the right direction.

The more you know about the sometimes strange way that things work in Portugal, the easier it is to settle down and enjoy this lovely, hospitable country and its delightfully kind and generous people.

2. A Place in the Sun

As you can see from a map, this is not a very big country.

Draw an imaginary line across the middle of England, starting at the mouth of the Humber and travelling west towards the border with Wales, taking in the counties of Lincoln, Nottingham, Leicester, Stafford and Shropshire. Ignore Wales, but include the county of Monmouth and you have an area south of your line which is almost exactly that of mainland Portugal: 35,500 square miles, or one-sixth of the Iberian Peninsula.

Portugal is packed with history and with the legacies of those who have lived here since the country was first inhabited —in 7000 BC or thereabouts. Not to mention those who came, saw and conquered for a while: the Celts, Phoenicians, Romans, Vandals and Visigoths, and the Moors, who were here for five hundred years and left their indelible imprint on southern Portugal. The Spaniards ruled for sixty inglorious years and left nothing much behind them, except a strong aversion by the Portuguese to being lumped together with their neighbours and spoken to in Spanish. The French were here briefly—until they were persuaded to leave by the Duke of Wellington, whose presence can be seen across the country from the lines of Torres Vedras to the string of fortified towns facing the Spanish border.

And what an amazing variety of scenery, climate and living conditions is crammed into this small space. Unless your idea of the perfect place to live is a concrete jungle, tropical rain forest or arid desert, you will almost certainly find what you are looking for in Portugal.

It has lush vine-clad valleys and sun-baked prairies. Rice paddies and ski slopes. Sub-tropical gardens and icy plateaux. Cork forests, citrus groves, neatly terraced hillsides, wide sandy beaches. Fishing villages, farming villages, isolated mountain communities and tranquil little towns that have been standing quietly in the sun since Roman times. Squat whitewashed cottages and stately homes. Brash modern developments and cattle ranches. Flossy resorts and wind-swept plains. Bleak rocky promontories inhabited only by seabirds, and cities like Lisbon that have managed to combine the old and the new without spoiling either. Ancient churches whose steeples wear storks' nests, and more picture-postcard palaces than you would believe possible. One was advertised for sale quite recently. Less than an hour's drive out of Lisbon, it came complete with deer park, oil press, chapter house, church, riding ring and many more palatial extras, all for a mere £620,000 o.n.o. A veritable snip, at less than £5,000 an acre—which was the current price of an empty field in this area.

Along the five-hundred-mile coastline, west and south, the climate is temperate. Dry and Mediterranean in the south, with the winters becoming progressively damper as you wend your way north from Cape St Vincent past Lisbon and Oporto (Porto, to the Portuguese) up to the province of Minho across the river from Galicia in western Spain. The further inland and eastward you go, the more extreme the climate becomes. In the north-eastern mountains of Trás-os-Montes province, in Beira Alta and the Alentejo plains, the winters can be cruelly cold and the summers unrelentingly hot.

The most densely populated of Portugal's eleven provinces are, inevitably and logically, coastal ones. Estremadura, which contains both Lisbon and the big industrial port city of Setúbal; Douro, where Oporto has been an important business centre since the days of the Romans; and Minho, the northernmost coastal province. By contrast, the southern coastal province of the Algarve is practically empty for most of the year, with fewer than 350,000 inhabitants to share its 2,000 square miles. At the height of the tourist season, of course, it is another matter. From June to September the seaside towns and villages seethe with humanity, and the roads are thick with cars and campers sporting foreign number-plates.

When it comes to choosing a permanent home in Portugal,

the sun-starved Britons and other north Europeans tend to congregate along or close to the coast. In the Algarve, where they can be reasonably sure of enjoying three thousand hours' sunshine a year. In the Lisbon area, on the Estoril coast and in the lower part of Estremadura, where the weather is rated ideal and where proximity to the attractions of Lisbon is an added bonus.

There is also a sizeable British population in Oporto, but they go more often to work than to play or sit in the sun. In spite of the nervous departure of business at the time of the Revolution, there are still plenty of British and foreign companies in Oporto—not counting the famous port wine industry which, as everyone knows, was originally developed by the English.

It is oddly difficult to obtain exact figures for the British population resident in Portugal, partly because the word "resident" is hard for the authorities to define. Anyone who comes to work here on, say, a two-year contract would take out official residence and therefore be as resident on paper as those of us who fully intend to end our days in Portugal. The British Embassy says it has no way of differentiating between these two categories.

Then, too, there are bound to be Britons who have decided to live for ever in Portugal but who have made their homes away from the popular expatriate areas. They may not even have visited Her Majesty's official representatives in this country: the Consular Section of the British Embassy in Lisbon and the Consulates in Oporto, Figueira da Foz, and Portimão in the Algarve. There are certainly people who forget to make their annual pilgrimage to the Consulate to have their passports re-stamped, and undoubtedly plenty who leave the country for reasons of their own without informing either the Portuguese or the British authorities.

One way and another, perhaps it is not surprising that figures for residents vary from seven thousand or so (the British Embassy) to twelve thousand (an English-language publication in Portugal).

In any event, quite a few Britons have decided that Portugal is a very good place to be.

Now it is unlikely that anyone reading this is starting from scratch, with no idea where they may want to live in Portugal. All the same and although this is not supposed to be a guide-book, it might be worth taking a quick look at the country from north to south, not necessarily province by province, but in zones—north, central and south—the way the Portuguese weather forecasters slice it up.

Technically, I suppose, such a look really ought to include what the Portuguese refer to as the Adjacent Islands— Madeira and the Azores. But for our purposes they do not seem adjacent enough. The nine-island archipelago of the Azores is in mid-Atlantic, almost as close to Newfoundland as it is to Portugal, and Madeira is a good five hundred miles south of Lisbon, off the coast of Morocco. Let's stick to the mainland.

The Wine-producing North

Starting at the top left-hand corner, the verdant wine-producing province of Minho has short, sunny summers and winters that are wet but not unduly cold. Trout-filled rivers and streams lace the landscape, which, where it is not intensely cultivated, is well forested. Wines grow everywhere, even up trees and lamp-posts, for this is where they make Portugal's famous "green" wines.

This is a province of pious, hard-working people, of old traditions, splendid country houses, picturesque villages and beautiful towns.

Braga, the provincial capital and ecclesiastical centre, is large and lovely, with hibiscus-lined streets. Viana do Castelo, on the mouth of the Lima river, is a prosperous city and popular resort. Guimarães was Portugal's twelfth-century capital, a lively, colourful town that is now the centre of the linen and lace trade.

If you really want to get away from it all, the north-eastern province of Trás-os-Montes (literally, "Behind the Mountains") is about as isolated as you can get. Quite untouched by tourism, this large and rugged area is not even mentioned in some travel books, which may or may not be a good thing for the people who live there. This too is wine-growing country, and the purple port wine grapes grow in the Douro river valleys, providing seasonal work for the local people. Up on the cold mountain plateaux they harvest barley and chestnuts. Rural living is simple in Trás-os-Montes, not to say primitive in some remote areas.

But Vila Real, the largest town, is an attractive one, with quiet ways and an abundance of sixteenth- and seventeenth-century houses. Miranda do Douro and medieval Bragança, being so close to the border and cut off from the rest of Portugal, have a Spanish air about them and seem several centuries behind the times.

Back on the coast, Oporto is the capital of Douro province, Portugal's second city and the closest you will come to an urban rat-race in this wonderfully civilized country. It's all go, go, go in Oporto, and its people are extremely proud of the bustle, efficiency and prosperity. "Coimbra sings," they say somewhat smugly, "Braga prays, Lisboa shows off, and Porto works." They may have a point. It is a wealthy city, off the usual tourist track, with many elegant buildings, its Stock Exchange, museums, monuments, fine restaurants and a lovely lacy bridge over the Douro that was designed by Alexandre Eiffel, no less. Another bridge, the Ponte de Dom Luis, connects Oporto with the port-wine suburb of Vila Nova de Gaia, where close to thirty manufacturers keep their supplies of port wine in long, low "lodges".

The Douro countryside is beautiful, as it is almost everywhere in the north, and enough rain falls here in winter to prevent the average Englishman becoming homesick. Summers are sunny and more than a little humid.

Further down the coast and still in the northern zone, Aveiro in Beira Litoral is an ancient city surrounded by lagoons, canals and saltpans, famous for succulent eels and luscious egg-yolk sweets. Almost due east, Viseu in Beira Alta is a quiet and charming country town with the remains of a Roman encampment on its outskirts and a museum devoted to the works of the sixteenth-century painter Vasco Fernandes (Grão Vasco). To the east, Guarda is the highest, coldest town in Portugal, a fortified city built by Dom Sancho I in 1197 and used by Wellington as one of his bases during the Peninsular War.

So much, very briefly, for Portugal's gloriously scenic and un-touristy north country.

Central Portugal

The central zone takes in the southern part of Beira Litoral as well as the province of Estremadura in the west and, moving east, the provinces of Beira Baixa and Ribatejo and the northern part of Alto Alentejo.

The best-known city in this area must be Coimbra, the steep, cobblestoned home of one of Europe's oldest universities, on the banks of the Mondego river. What a delightful place to live: historic and romantic, full of life and music; its climate is comfortable, with the summer heat tempered by Atlantic breezes, and winters that are chilly without ever deteriorating into snow. In spring and summer the tour buses roll in—and rightly, for this is one of Portugal's showplaces.

In the next-door province of Beira Baixa, splendidly gardened Castelo Branco sits close to the Spanish border, with the farmlands of the Tagus valley (Tejo, on Portuguese maps) at its feet and a backdrop of mountains behind. To its north, Covilhã is the heart of the wool industry and a rapidly developing centre for the winter sports and summer hiking on the slopes of Serra da Estrêla. South of Castelo Branco, across the Tagus, Portalegre in the Northern Alentejo is an episcopal city surrounded by Roman roads and footbridges, reminders that this was once an important and well-populated centre.

These days it is the western half of the central zone that is well populated. The broad Tagus valley in the province of Ribatejo ("Beside the Tagus") is cattle country, with fertile farmland and large estates. Santarém, the provincial capital, is one of the oldest and most historic cities in Portugal, an administrative centre under Julius Caesar, an impregnable stronghold in Moorish times, captured by Crusaders in 1147.

Tomar on the river Nabão is becoming gradually more industrialized and is noted mainly for its great convent-castle of the Knights Templar. Towards the Tagus mouth, Vila Franca de Xira is Portugal's answer to Spanish Pamplona, if such a thing were needed, and the big annual event is the summer bull-run (*Festa da Colete Encarnado*) down the main street of the town.

And so to the coast and Estremadura, which stretches from the area just north of Leiria down through Lisbon to Setúbal on the Sado estuary.

Those who live there say that the part of Portugal that lies in and around the capital provides the best of all possible worlds. A benign and sunny climate, though admittedly damp in winter. Magnificent beaches. Good roads and rail services from the centre of Lisbon to the fashionable resorts and popular residential areas. Excellent shopping. Reliable services. Entertainment, social and sporting activities, and a large cosmopolitan community where English is widely spoken.

Estremadura is a beautiful province, filled with fascinating towns and villages, and with marvellous monuments to the highspots in Portugal's history. Óbidos, the lovely walled city that was for more than six centuries the traditional wedding gift of the kings of Portugal to their queens. Torres Vedras, the chain of 150 hilltop fortresses that were Wellington's famous line of defence against the French; historically exciting, but today a little dull as a town. Batalha with its huge honey-coloured abbey, built by Dom João I to commemorate Portugal's fourteenth-century independence from Spain. Sintra, beloved by Byron and just about everyone else who has seen this lushly green and wooded town, where Portuguese royalty used to spend its summers.

The stretch of coastline that includes Estoril and Cascais looks and feels like the south of France, with palm trees and landscaped gardens, casinos and lavish villas, and expensive hotels looking out over the Atlantic. It is posh and plush and was, until they started to die off, packed with exiled European royalty.

Across the estuary from the Portuguese Riviera, Palmela is a pretty little town with an imposing castle in the Arrábida hills. Setúbal on the mouth of the Sado river is Portugal's third port city, quite heavily industrialized; the old town, though, is still attractive. Sesimbra, a pleasant fishing-cum-resort town overlooking the bay and sheltered by the Serra da Arrábida, seems remote from the twentieth-century bustle of the big cities, yet is only a short drive from Setúbal and the capital.

To some residents of this Portuguese paradise, the country probably stops right there, and there must be many who have never ventured from Lisbon over the great Ponte do 25 de Abril, the longest suspension bridge in Europe, and taken the road to the south.

The sunny South

The southern zone is made up of the lower part of Alto Alentejo, Baixa Alentejo and, over the mountains, the Algarve.

In the east of the underpopulated Alentejo, Estremoz is a rather beautiful garrison town built mainly of marble, dominated by a hilltop castle and famous for its pottery. A few kilometres south, Évora is the most important Alentejo city: walled, with winding narrow streets, glorious gardens, museums, churches and archaeological finds that include the well-known Roman Temple of Diana. Beja, in the heart of the wheat belt, was founded by Julius Caesar, fortified by the Moors and is a pretty, sprawling town today, guarded by giant grain elevators.

Grimly cold in winter and quite ridiculously hot in summer, life is hard for the people of this large and inhospitable-looking province. Seen from a car on the way to or from Lisbon, it is desolate and endless, the monotony broken from time to time by cork forests, small groups of cottages huddled together and the occasional dusty town. Even the Alentejo coastline is empty—though how long it will stay that way is anyone's guess. From Setúbal down to Sines and on into the Algarve, there is practically nothing to see at the moment but sea. And miles of sandy beaches.

The Algarve beaches on the other hand and the other side of the mountains, are that province's great attraction, both for the tourists and for many of the foreigners who come to settle. Beautiful beaches and the much-advertised sunny, warm climate.

Having said that, I am reminded that not so long ago there was a sudden biting cold spell, and Algarveans were stunned to see snow on their side of the Monchique mountains, for the first time in almost thirty years. It lasted only one day, which the local children enjoyed no end, and anyone on the coast who could find an excuse and some transport went dashing into the hills to see this remarkable phenomenon for themselves.

Even in this small province there are changes of scenery and climate.

Between the mountains and the beaches there are forests of cork, mimosa and eucalyptus, groves of citrus, almond and olive; large man-made lakes that irrigate the rice- and fruit-growing areas; small towns and villages, many of them centuries old, that seem to grow smaller each year as the coastal population gets larger.

The southern coast, about a hundred miles from Cape St Vincent to the Guadiana river, a ferry-ride from Spain, is twice divided: in two parts by its climate, and into three parts by its population.

The eastern half is markedly warmer at any time of year than the western half, where the Atlantic winds can and do come howling in over the Sagres Peninsula. It is pleasant in summer, when the winds drop from gales down to cooling breezes, but it can be surprisingly nippy in January and February, even though the sun still shines.

This southern coast, and particularly the central section, is holiday land. Between Faro and Lagos, the most westerly Algarve city of any size, you will find the names that feature on charter-flight luggage-labels. Smart developments like Vale do Lobo and Vilamoura. Erstwhile fishing villages like Quarteira, Albufeira, Carvoeiro and Praia da Rocha, now fast disappearing among the villas, hotels and high-rise apartment buildings. This is where the Algarve action is.

The eastern third, from Faro to Vila Real de Santo António, is all quiet farmlands and fishing communities, grazing sheep, almond trees and Day-Glo oranges. There is one ancient and beautiful little town along the way, Tavira; and another rather unattractive one with a spectacular beach, almost at the end of Portugal. Other than that, not much to disturb the peace.

The western third is also quiet and, despite the developers, less blemished than the central section by tall and inappropriate slabs of concrete. The seaside villages that have expanded to accommodate the tourists have managed, on the whole, to do so gracefully and to retain at least some of their personality. And although Prince Henry the Navigator's port city of Lagos grows bigger every year, it is still the most attractive one on the coast.

It can't last, of course. But at the moment it is still possible to walk the length of Lagos Bay, where Nelson used to park the entire British fleet, and see hardly a soul in the winter time. Or to hike for miles over cliffs and countryside—from Lagos to Cape St Vincent, if you have the stamina—without meeting another human being. As for the west Algarve coast, from Cape St Vincent up to the Alentejo border, the people there still stop what they are doing to watch an aeroplane fly overhead. If it were not for the cars and the television aerials, you would find it hard to believe that anything had happened here in the last hundred years.

Come to that, one gets the feeling that the whole Algarve was dragged reluctantly into the twentieth century only a couple of decades ago, when the bridge over the Tagus and the airport at Faro were opened at much the same time in the mid-1960s. Until then, it was a long, hard trek to the southern province either by car along indifferent roads or by train that stopped at every lamp-post. A few hardy and determined Britons made it, but since there were plenty of sunny beaches on their own doorstep, few Lisboans bothered. In its own quiet way, the Algarve was almost as remote as that other province "Behind the Mountains" and as foreign as North Africa —which it still resembles in many ways.

Anyone who is thinking of moving to Portugal without much money would probably be wise to stay away from the popular tourist centres and those with a well-entrenched foreign community. Foreigners, whether transient or permanent, usually require what rural Portuguese would regard as outrageously expensive services and facilities. Foreigners make a beeline for the coast and, as in any sunny country, coastal property here is at a premium in the more favoured areas.

Before tourism took hold, southern Algarve farmers were quite delighted to unload their unproductive bits of barren clifftop onto anyone silly enough to buy them. The early foreign settlers and those with an optimistic eye on the future paid only pennies per square metre for land that you could not buy today for £50 and more. The buyers went away laughing —and the farmers laughed just as heartily, convinced that all foreigners were mad. Since those early 1960s, the Algarve farmers have become a great deal more sophisticated, especially where foreigners are concerned.

If your budget is small but you still want to live by the sea anywhere south of Lisbon, you will have to look along the undeveloped Alentejo and western Algarve coasts or, on the south coast, to the east of Faro. But cross Estrada Nacional 125, the Algarve's east-west highway, and only a few kilometres inland the prices are more reasonable. Looking at some current listings: a plot of land in a small and so far unspoilt fishing village in the eastern section can be had for £20 a square metre. Not too far away, on the other side of the main road, you can buy a square metre for just under £4. In neither case do you get any water or electricity on the land.

The further inland you go, the cheaper everything becomes. But if you tuck yourself well off the tourist track, you may have to learn to live without many of the amenities you have taken for granted all these years. Instead of putting your bin out for the dustmen to empty, you will probably have to tote your rubbish down the road to the municipal *lixo* box or dig a pit at the bottom of your garden for rubbish and have an all-consuming fire now and again. Instead of main drainage, you are more likely to have a *fossa*, a cesspool. You may or may not have any electricity. Your water may have to be pumped from a well, or even be delivered by truck and stored in a cistern.

And if you have chosen to live in a small, exclusively Portuguese community, you can be quite sure that the local shop will stock only those items that the Portuguese know and need. You will not see any of the high-priced foods that foreigners find essential, even on holiday—things like bottled mayonnaise, fancy breakfast cereals, imported cheese and expensive brands of fancy English tea.

Not too many British people relish the idea of moving into a totally foreign environment where nobody can speak their language. Only the young, adaptable and adventurous are that brave. But we have met people who took the plunge, and they never regretted it for a moment; for the Portuguese, unlike the British, seem genuinely pleased to welcome foreigners into their lives.

One young British couple spent several extraordinarily happy years in a nothing-type Alentejo village where nobody had even seen an *estrangeiro* before, much less tried to communicate with one. The local people, they told us, were the kindest and most generous neighbours they had ever had. Most of the foreign residents we have talked to tell more or less the same story. They came to Portugal for a holiday, loved it and decided that this was where they wanted to live.

Not always in their original holiday spot. Some people spent their first Portuguese holiday in the Estoril-Cascais region, decided to explore further afield and ended by making their home in the south. Others enjoyed an Algarve holiday but felt that, like New York, though it was a nice place to visit, they did not want to live there. Too provincial. They found their happiness closer to Lisbon.

To be fair, there have also been a few people who, after living here for a number of years, became suddenly overwhelmed with a longing for Britain and departed. No harm done, except perhaps financially. But it is as well to take a long, hard look at yourself before pulling up stakes and moving to another country. Some people are simply not born to emigrate.

Whether you make an instant decision about where you want to live in Portugal or whether you take your time exploring, once you have picked that place, do visit it as often as possible before committing yourself, particularly if you are proposing to move from a large town or city into, say, a small fishing village or a seaside resort. You will not only be changing countries, which is traumatic enough, but you will also be changing your whole way of life.

What's more, your new home may well have several different faces, and you would be wise to see them all.

When you first visit that idyllic fishing village, it is very likely in summer, when everything is bright and cheerful, just as the brochure promised. If there are surprises, they are usually pleasant ones. And if they are not so pleasant, there is always a hotel or property manager or a tour company representative who will rush to put things right.

Go back out of season and you may hardly recognize the place. The deliciously cool villa which was such a welcome relief from the hot summer sun can be cold and damp in winter. In some of the Algarve resorts, where the houses are built in the Arab style against the sun, there are days when it is definitely warmer out of doors than in. You will probably find that most—if not all—those jolly little local bars and restaurants are closed. Having worked like maniacs all summer, staff and owners take their holidays in the winter. Bus and postal services may have been cut back for the off-season. You may be up to your knees in mud after the much-needed winter rain. And if it rains during your stay, all the electricity in the village will probably go off. None of which matters in the long run, providing you are forewarned.

We made several out-of-season visits before we came to live here, and saw this village at its bleak and soggy worst. All the same, our first winter storm took us completely by surprise.

We had gone to bed one October night, after a gloriously warm and summery day, to be woken in the small hours by something that sounded remarkably like a replay of the London Blitz. Gale-force winds were roaring in off the sea and straight into our sitting-room, battering the large french windows and tossing the sturdy patio furniture around as though it was made of balsa wood. The noise was incredible, what with the wind bansheeing down the chimneys and the furniture bouncing and crashing from wall to wall. No electricity, naturally. We sat huddled in blankets, candle in one hand and brandy in the other, waiting for the windows to come crashing in on us and wishing we had never read John D. MacDonald's book about hurricanes.

The storm raged for three ear-splitting, mind-bending days, and then, just as we were either becoming immune to the noise or going slightly deaf, it stopped as suddenly as it had started.

Another lesson learned the hard way.

From then on, as soon as the holidaymakers began to thin out, we began to remove plants, furniture and anything else that could get blown about on the balcony. If, after all that, we ever go through a winter without at least one good storm, we feel quite put out.

Another thing to consider while you are pondering a seaside resort: how do you feel about spending half the year surrounded by people on holiday? Unless you move here from a British resort (and not many people do that) you may find it rather strange. If your next-door apartment or villa is rented out for the summer, will it bother you to have constantly changing neighbours? Are you prepared to put up with slamming doors, party-giving, the noise of people lurching home at dawn from the discos? Not that these things will necessarily happen—but you never know.

This was yet another thing that we had never even thought about until we moved into the apartment and found that our neighbours changed every fortnight. By which time, it was a bit late. Fortunately, we greatly enjoy both the coming-and-going summers and the solitary winters, when there can be only one other resident family in this block. We could equally well have hated both summer and winter.

Friends in another resort village are not nearly so pleased at the prospect of summer and the influx of visitors. Though they live in a large villa far from the centre of things, the neighbouring house is big enough to be rented to a rugger team or a great gaggle of friends—and it often is. There are times when the all-night pool-parties, and the multi-decibel music, crashing of glasses and raucous laughter can be heard for miles.

Visit your prospective new home as often as you can, so you see it in all its moods. Look at the people who spend their holidays there. Sporting types and night-owls can make for a noisy summer. If you prefer to sleep at night, seek out a village or resort that attracts families with small children.

Look at the year-round residents and get to know as many as you can, both British and Portuguese. The more friends you have when you actually get here, the easier life will be. No matter how many books you read on the subject, you will still need plenty of practical help when you start living in Portugal, and anyone who has been here for a year or two will be delighted to give it.

The last decision in this first phase is, I suppose, to decide what you want to live in.

Apartments, condominiums and villa developments are found in profusion along the south coast and, to a lesser degree in the Lisbon-Estoril-Cascais area. If you are browsing through the advertisements and find the ugly word "urbanisation", that is a development.

You will also see a number of advertisements about time-sharing, which is relatively new here and which is being heavily promoted. So far, nobody we have spoken to has invested in a time-share apartment with a view to using their annual week or weeks as a first step towards moving permanently to Portugal. This is strictly a holiday deal and, as such, is not really what we're talking about.

On the subject of apartments, though, you are unlikely to find many blocks of flats in villages that are off the popular tourist track. Look in the towns, if this is what you want.

I really don't know how helpful it is to tell you what you can expect to pay at this time, in the winter of 1986–7. By the time you get here, or even start any serious house-hunting, prices will almost certainly have gone up in the tourist areas. On the other hand, at the rate building is going on along the southern coast, there may well be even more choice than there is now.

At the moment, you will probably not find anything very much in a popular coastal area under £20,000, particularly if you want more than one bedroom.

There is a one-bedroomed apartment in a prestigious Algarve development going for £30,000. Another furnished one with two bedrooms in the centre of a busy southern resort town is listed at £32,000, only a kilometre away from the very beautiful beach. More reasonable in price is the ground floor apartment in the Oporto area, which has a conservatory and a one-car garage and is listed at only £24,000.

Fifty thousand pounds or thereabouts will buy you a converted farmhouse in the Algarve foothills. Or a delightful-sounding cottage near Sintra, with three bedrooms. Double your money and you can have a huge house with a pool, plus an acre of land and a spectacular view just to the south of Lisbon.

If you have money to spend on your Portuguese home, you can live splendidly. If you are not so well off, you can still find what you want, more or less where you want it—but you may have to look harder.

3. Keeping in Touch

Ease of communication, both with your neighbours and with the outside world, may be something to take into consideration when you are looking around for the ideal spot to settle in Portugal.

In the Lisbon and Oporto areas, where there are sizeable English-speaking communities and the telephones work rather better than they do in the Algarve, there should be very little difficulty in making yourself understood and keeping in touch. Along the coastal stretch of the southernmost province, plenty of English is spoken in the towns and resorts, though not necessarily in the rural areas or along the undeveloped west coast. If you elect to live in the middle of the underpopulated Alentejo or in a Trás-os-Montes hamlet, you may very well be the only *estrangeiro* for miles around, with no choice but to buckle down and master at least a little Portuguese if you want to communicate with anyone outside your own household.

Learning the language

It is, as you know, an extraordinarily difficult language. The only one, a Sitwell once said, where Tottenham Court Road comes out as a single syllable. And he was referring, as far as anyone knows, to Lisboan Portuguese, which is crystal-clear compared to some of the provincial dialects. Nevertheless, the Portuguese claim that their language is spoken by something like 150 million people around the world—including any number of Britons who have made their home in Portugal.

Some Brits do a lot better than others.

It is important that you make an effort to learn at least a smattering of the language. For one thing, it is only good manners, since you are a guest in this country. For another, it is frustrating to hear people prattling around you and not be able to join in. Even more important, it is vital to have an idea what is going on. At the moment, with Portugal fighting her way out of an economic shambles, new fiscal and other regulations can appear without warning, and it is as well to be aware of them.

Soon after we settled here and before we had learned to keep an eye, however uneducated, on television or press, it was suddenly decreed that all cars would wear mud-flaps. Luckily someone in the village brought this to our notice, and we were able to get ourselves flapped before we got fined. Had we been paying attention, we would not have had to rely on the local grapevine.

Portuguese is not all that difficult to read, especially if you have a knowledge of French, Spanish or even Latin. With patience and a good dictionary, you can struggle through the lead stories of a local paper and get at least the gist, if not the nuances of the news.

It took us a long time to lay our hands on a really good Portuguese dictionary, one of the *Dicionárias Escolares*. For years we had to make do with the trusty green pocket Collins, a Collins phrase-book and a great doorstop of a dictionary published in Oporto which contained the most extraordinary English words and insisted that "foots" was a noun. But it did tell us that the Portuguese word for daughter-in-law can also mean a water-wheel, that a *fossa* can be either a cesspool or a dimple, and that if one is careless with gender the Portuguese for "sort" or "kind" can emerge as "strumpet" and cause much confusion. The British bookshops should be able to produce something more useful than that. Keep an eye open.

And while you're at it, see if you can find the newly published volume of *Português Fundamental* and its companion grammar. Fourteen years in the making and produced by the Centre of Linguistic Studies at the Lisbon Faculty of Arts, *Português Fundamental* reduces the language down to a mere 2,200 words—enough, they say, to carry on a sensible conversation at any social level.

It would also be worth investing in some Portuguese lessons before you get here, because the language does not sound the way it looks. Even that crash course for businessmen, available in London, would be a help.

With hindsight—and there has been plenty of that over the last few years—we wish now we had spent less time grumbling about having to speak French in Quebec and more time finding someone to teach us a little everyday Portuguese. Linguaphone and Berlitz are all very well, but once you are actually living in Portugal, you will probably find it more important to be able to discuss the price of fish than the fact that the teacher's book is on the table.

Fortunately, all the Portuguese people we have met have been unfailingly kind and helpful about our struggles with their language. They hardly laugh at all, though, like the British abroad, they are inclined to believe that, if they shout loud enough, we will eventually understand what they are saying. But they smile rather than sneer at our howlers, correct us gently and seem genuinely pleased when, after much floundering, we manage to make ourselves understood. From which you will gather that we are still very far from fluent, to our shame.

Even if you arrive knowing only please-and-thank-you Portuguese, you will gradually pick up a few phrases by osmosis. The two most useful and quickly learned are "*mais ou menos*", which means "more or less" and can apply to the state of your health as well as to a price, weight or measurement. "*Não faz mal*" covers everything from "never mind" or "don't worry about it" to "what the hell", depending on the tenor of the conversation.

To hasten the learning process and get a grounding in grammar, you could enrol in one of the many language schools that can be found in Portuguese cities of any size. One, based in Lisbon, offers a month's intensive course of ten hours a week, at the end of which you should be able to hold your own.

There are a number of smaller organizations that promise to teach you just enough Portuguese to get by on, all in a matter of hours. There are private individuals who tutor on a one-to-one basis or who will instruct small groups. Some of our most enthusiastic teachers have been the lady who comes to lend a hand in the flat and the children from the village school, who find it hilarious that we can't speak their language.

The quickest and most painless way to learn Portuguese, we are assured by some of our most bilingual friends, is to live with a Portuguese national. But this is not always practical.

Television helps

. . . Or so we told each other earnestly before we broke all our good resolutions and bought a black-and-white set for what seemed an enormous amount of money compared with British and Canadian prices. That was before colour came to Portugal in 1981. Since then, prices have dropped dramatically, and we are now the only people we know in the neighbourhood who are still colourless.

If you are the sort of person who has to see something written down before it makes any sense, television really is a boon. There are a surprising number of English and other foreign programmes in the course of a week, all with Portuguese sub-titles. After eight years' worth of films ancient and modern and some quite surprisingly up-to-date British and American shows, Portuguese now makes much more sense.

It was not until I was idly watching a Popeye cartoon on Children's Hour that the Portuguese for "spinach" finally registered. Until I saw it in print, it had sounded like a smothered sneeze.

People say the best way to achieve an understanding of spoken Portuguese is to start with the first episode of one of the popular and almost interminable Brazilian soap operas on television, and stick with it to the bitter end. It takes intestinal fortitude, but the Brazilian accent is much easier on the foreign ear than the Lisboan, clearer and nothing like as fast. (The soaps themselves are a bit Barbara Cartland, but excellently done and remarkably easy to follow, if you pay attention, because everything is so broadly played.)

Apart from entertainment in a variety of languages, it is almost essential to have television because through it you learn the important facts of life in Portugal today. Sudden announcements concerning increased prices, deadlines for tax payments, new regulations about cars, or threatened strikes all appear on the box. Even before you see it written up on the screen, you soon learn to pick key words such as *sindicado* (trade union) and *greve* (strike) out of the air and gear yourself for a short hiatus in some essential service.

Commercials, too, take on a new importance when you first come to Portugal. Unless you are faithfully studying

Portuguese papers, you probably won't know about new products until they appear in the local shops. Even then, you may not be entirely sure what to do with them. And TV commercials do help you learn about Portuguese brand-names, which, if you have not done any holiday housekeeping here, can be a bit bewildering at the start.

I was delighted to discover that the soap pads I knew in Britain as Brillo and had eventually learned to call SOS in Canada were known in Portugal as Bravo, and I would not have to resort to scouring with sand to get saucepans clean. It was something I had not even thought about until I was faced with a scrambled-eggy pan a day or two after we arrived here.

Radio contact

Obviously you can get all this information—from strikes to soap pads—from the radio. Some people find that the best way to soak up the language is to stay permanently tuned to one of the several Portuguese stations.

I wish we were dedicated enough to do this, if only because there is so much good music on the Portuguese air. But the lure of BBC World Service is too strong and, although reception in our area is less than perfect for large chunks of the day, that is where our ancient radio stays tuned.

Mais ou menos. With Casablanca only three hundred miles to our south, we are swamped here by broadcasts in Arabic and French, and by electronic muezzins calling the faithful to prayer just as we settle to hear the news from London. There are days when we are convinced that all the British Isles have sunk without trace; all we can find, no matter how hard we twiddle, are transmissions from Russia, Australia, Taiwan, Ecuador, China and the good old Voice of America, which comes in loud and clear when we least need it.

A really good short-wave radio is a must for anyone who wants to keep in touch the easy way, without having to stay awake until midnight—when even our antique will pick up Radio Four with no trouble or interference.

With a machine like a Grundig Satellit and a good aerial, you can get the BBC World Service on several short-wave frequencies twenty-four hours a day. But those frequencies change and your best source of up-to-date information is the BBC's *London Calling*, a monthly publication which lists those currently in use and which you can sometimes pick up at the British Consulate. It is also available on subscription from BBC World Service, PO Box 76, Bush House, London WC2B 4PH.

Taxes are levied on both radio and television sets, but the one for radio turns up unexpectedly. Part of the money that goes to pay your electricity bill is syphoned off for this purpose, on the grounds, presumably, that if you are rich enough to have electricity, you are rich enough to have a radio, and bright enough to plug it in. We only discovered this after we had spent a small fortune on batteries, believing we were conserving energy.

Television sets are taxed. Very slightly by British standards and, until recently, rather haphazardly.

When we got our set, taxation operated on the honour system. You were supposed to get a form from the post office, fill it in and pay 365 escudos (about £3.50 in those days) for a year's viewing. But even that was easier said than done.

A week after our TV was installed we trotted into town to pay up. The tax was, we were told sternly, only payable in January.

Come January, we joined the long line of hopeful tax-payers—only to find that the post office had run out of forms. It was made very clear by the harassed lady behind the bars that she wished we would all go away. So we did.

In 1982 the authorities initiated a new system which involved registering the purchase of a TV set before it left the shop. And a direct-mail campaign announcing the inevitable increase in the tax with, as a blow-softener, an amnesty on all delinquent viewers in honour of the Pope's visit to Portugal.

There was a nationwide sigh of relief, and the tax money came rolling in.

The written word

Still on the subject of learning the language: it makes sense to persevere with local papers and magazines. They will not do much for your pronunciation, but every little helps.

The best-read magazine, judging by the difficulty we have in buying a copy each week, is *TV Guia*, Portugal's *TV Times*. We find this most useful. Not so much for the programme listings—which should never be taken as gospel because programmes can change without warning—as for the relatively easy reading matter. We have learned more than we care to know about the personal lives of the cast of *Dallas* from this publication.

A useful source of information for expatriates is the *Anglo-Portuguese News*, a well-established English-language weekly that is published just outside Lisbon and widely circulated throughout Portugal. *APN* appears every Thursday and costs sixty escudos in the newspaper shops and kiosks. If you want to begin keeping up with the news before you leave Britain, write to *APN* at Ave. de São Pedro 17, 2765 Monte Estoril, Estremadura with £36 for a year's airmail subscription. If you want to have it mailed to your Portuguese address, the annual subscription is 3,500 escudos. This is by far the most reliable of the English-language publications in this country.

Incidentally, if you have been here on holiday, you will know that day-old English newspapers are available in the places where British people congregate. They cost the earth, and the Sundays arrive without their colour supplements. Sometimes the papers do not arrive at all, owing to bad weather or airport strikes, and you can hear the howls of disappointment all over town as crossword and comic-strip addicts are deprived of their treat. But the day you decide you can do quite nicely without yesterday's news at the cost of a fair-to-middling bottle of wine, you will know that your roots have started going down in Portugal. It is a pretty good feeling.

Even so, you will still want to communicate with the rest of the world, and have the rest of the world communicate with you.

The Post Office

The Portuguese postal service is surprisingly good. True, the price of stamps goes steadily up, as it does everywhere else. True, too, the service can be disrupted by transport strikes. And there are certainly times when it seems that it is quicker for a letter to travel the fifteen hundred miles from Britain to this village than to cover the six or so miles from our nearest town. But, generally speaking and despite the odd grumble, the service is better than we ever expected and much more amiable than some we could mention.

Until a few years ago there was a real post office in this village, complete with a very public telephone and a permanent queue of people wanting to use it. Then it suddenly disappeared. Not, as rumour had it, because it had run out of stamps, but because the lease on the building had expired. Since then, we have relied on a mobile post van which rolls up on weekdays and deals with mail, money orders, pension cheques and the like. With the van and our delightful motor-biking postman, we feel we are very well served.

The only time the system collapses is when the postman takes his annual month's holiday. Faced with a fistful of letters with foreign names on them, and a route through a rabbit-warren of a village with no street names or house numbers, last year's replacement postman lost his nerve and dumped the lot in a tour company office. It was two weeks before the mail was discovered, by which time all the British residents were panicking and several telephones had been cut off for non-payment of bills.

Understandably, some people who live in rural or semi-rural areas prefer to take a box (*Apartado*) in the nearest post office. If there is one available, the *Chefe* explains that it is yours on a yearly or half-yearly basis for 910 escudos a year and gives you three copies of the application form to fill in and sign. Your signature, however, must be verified at the official notary's office before the forms can be returned to the post office and you are given your key.

The business of getting your signature verified is quite simple if you have already acquired your *Bilhete de Identidade* (see Chapter 9). Produce the blue card and the forms and someone in the office will countersign, enter the information in a large book, ask you for 30 escudos and that is that.

If you are organizing an *Apartado* before you have actually become a resident of Portugal, you will not yet own an identity card. In that case, take your passport to the notarial office and your signature will be verified from that.

Many people say it is well worth while having a signature lodged with the notary, because it allows friends or employees to do business on their behalf. It saves time if they send a signed document from abroad, or if their maid takes the monthly payments to the Social Security office (see Chapter 12). All you have to do is round up a couple of people whose signatures are already registered. They will attest to yours in front of the notary, who will register it and give you a numbered card to that effect.

Telephones
As well as delivering mail and kindly taking away letters to be posted when we missed the van, our postman also used to present us with the monthly phone bills. He then stood clucking sympathetically while we rustled up the money or, more often, the family cheque book.

It is generally admitted, even by the Portuguese, that until about 1984 or so a phone in this corner of the country was a mixed blessing. Lisboans are probably still being rude about the Algarve telephone system, which they regard as a bad joke, and insisting that it is quicker to get on a bus and go and talk to someone in Faro face-to-face than to get a call through to them. But this is no longer true. It has, touch wood, been several months since our phone went seriously out of order.

Coming from Canada, where even welfare recipients have telephones and all local calls are free, it never occurred to us that we might have to live without one. It was only when we had asked the builder's office to make our application that we learned that people in this area had been waiting ten years and more for a machine.

By sheer good luck we got ours in only three years—by which time we had become accustomed to leaving messages with people around the town, or simply trudging off to see whoever we wanted to speak to. In an emergency, we knew we could use the only private telephone in the village. Always supposing it was working. In those days, lines seemed to pack up with the first drop of rain, and a good windstorm was enough to put the whole system out of action for a week.

Since those early days there has been an enormous increase

in the number of phone installations all over the country and, in this province, a great improvement in technology. In Faro all the ladies with headphones have been replaced by the most modern automatic switching equipment, and every area now has its up-to-date exchange.

There is a rumour that we can now place a person-to-person call overseas, or reverse the charges on a call, just as they do in Lisbon. Frankly, we have never dared try anything quite so advanced. But we can dial directly to Britain and to most of the western world. It may take time, of course, to get what often seems to be the one and only line out of Portugal, but that is really no different from trying to make an overseas call in Britain, particularly if you are phoning during office hours or in the cheap rate period. On the other hand, you can some-times get through instantly to an overseas number—only to find that the line fades, crackles like cornflakes or disappears in mid-sentence. This, I know, can also happen anywhere in the world, but in Portugal it can be quite expensive trying to make yourself heard under these tiresome conditions.

Telephoning is a costly business in this country, no doubt about it. And oddly, it is a better bargain to phone overseas than to call long or even not-very-long distance in Portugal. At the moment, it is costing an enormous amount a minute to talk to anyone outside your own Area Code, and it makes no difference whether your telephone is one kilometre away from the dividing line or whether you are calling someone at the other end of the country.

Local calls are not cheap either. It took us three itemized bills to realize this and to break our North American habit of indulging in long, neighbourly matters. Coming from Britain, you will be much better trained.

A Portuguese telephone has some disconcerting character-istics. For example, it is often impossible to tell from your end whether the number you have dialled has been disconnected or is out of order or whether the owners are merely not at home. All you hear is the normal ringing tone. If, after a couple of tries, you decide that the house cannot possibly be empty—a call at 6 a.m. is often the clincher—their phone is obviously not making a sound and yours is lying. Dial the number listed in the phone book for Service (*Reparacões*) and struggle to report the matter in Portuguese.

It can also be quite difficult to get a dialling tone, certainly in the Algarve. There is a reassuring click when you lift the receiver, but after that—*nada*. Stony silence.

It does not help to hammer the buttons on the receiver rest, which is my husband's usual reaction. But you might try pushing the receiver buttons down and releasing them gently. This can sometimes coax the machine into behaving itself. If not, all you can do is wait a while and then try again. The silence may just be your own phone having a private fit of the vapours, or it may be a widespread nonsense—in which case, neither coaxing nor cursing will do any good.

When your own telephone goes on the blink, ask everyone within a five-kilometre radius to report it to *Reparacões*. The more complaints you can get registered, the quicker something will be done about it. The fault will either be fixed behind the scenes and after a while you will be back in business, or else a worried technician will turn up on the doorstep.

All of which sounds as though owning a Portuguese telephone is a full-time occupation. It is nothing of the sort, of course. It just works a bit differently from the one you have been used to.

Then there is the Portuguese telephone directory, which is also different. There are six of them, covering Continental Portugal, the islands of Madeira and the Azores, and each one comes with its Yellow Pages, which is very handy.

The first section of any directory is taken up with general information about how to use the phone, an incomprehensible table of charges (which are probably out of date before the directory gets off the press), the numbers to dial for this and that, and a massive index of every Portuguese telephone exchange. After which, you get to the first of the alphabetically arranged Areas in the book, with their Area Codes.

Our Southern Region (*Região Sul*) directory lists fourteen Areas which run geographically from Portalegre in the upper Alentejo north-east of Lisbon, down to the Algarve—which consists of three Areas: Tavira (Area Code 081), Faro (089) and Portimão (082). Tucked between the Areas of Faro and

Moura, in the right alphabetical spot, is a two-page spread headed "Lisboa" and giving a listing of the most important numbers in the capital.

At the start of each separate Area listing there is a page that tells you everything you need to know: a map of Portugal, another one of the Area in question with all the local exchanges carrying that Area Code, numbers to call for Enquiries, Service, Long-Distance Operators for home and abroad, Telegrams and so on. Turn the page and you'll find subscribers listed in the principal city (Portalegre, Faro, Tavira or wherever) and after that, subscribers in all the other Area exchanges, which are listed in alphabetical order.

All very logical, once you have found your way around.

Our first brush with the Algarve telephone system came only days after we arrived here, when we had to call the shipping agent in Lisbon. We braced ourselves with brandy and settled down to study the phone book.

It took us some time to work out where we were and what we had to do, but once that was established, we decided it was a doddle. All we had to do was dial the Area Code for Lisbon—01—and the shipper's number. Two days and a lot of wasted adrenalin later, somebody mentioned casually that at that time you had to dial "8" if you were trying to phone Lisbon from the Algarve. This does not apply any more, you'll be glad to hear. If you can get a dialling tone in the Algarve, just dial 01 for the capital.

It is easy enough to look up a number, providing you look under the right name. If a telephone subscriber moves to another address within the same Area Code, he can take his phone and phone number with him. And if he has any sense, he does just that. If he moves to a new Area, he has to go back to square one and apply for a new telephone, while his old one is theoretically reclaimed by the Post Office. However, it may take several years before his name, address and number are removed from the directory.

Should you be lucky enough to move into a house or an apartment with a working phone, keep quiet about it. Just pay all the bills that come addressed to the previous owner, or even the owner before that, and remember to tell everyone the relevant name, in case they forget the number and need to consult the phone book.

In spite of all this and the huge bills that appear every month, we would not be without our telephone. When it works, it is a lifeline to the family in Britain. When it doesn't, it serves to remind us how shamefully spoilt we were in Canada—two separate lines and four phones in one small house, for heaven's sake!—and how easy it is to take these things for granted.

To start the still somewhat protracted business of acquiring a telephone, apply to the Post Office. Then sit back and wait. Probably for about a year, these days, unless you need the phone for business purposes, or you are elderly and/or in poor health, in which case a doctor's certificate to that effect may speed things up.

Eventually a man appears to see if you have given up hope and, if not, to collect the large installation fee. In 1986 it was 9,000 escudos. By now it will certainly be more. You will then have another relatively short wait until the machine is installed, cheerfully and exactly where you want it.

If you need anything over and above a single phone, such as a bedroom extension or an extra-long cord, tell the man who comes with the installation bill. And mention it again when they come to put the telephone in. Once you are all connected up and everyone has gone away, it can take years to persuade them to come back and instal any extras.

While you are at it, think about having a *contador* fitted, a push-button meter that records the duration of a call in units. If you live in a small community where phones are scarce, it is only neighbourly to allow other people to use yours—and then you are into the awkward business of payment.

We have had some quite heated arguments with a Portu-guese neighbour who makes occasional calls to Lisbon. If she can get through, there is no telling how long her calls last because we disappear tactfully into another room. When we emerge, she tries to press handfuls of escudos on us and we try, as best we can, to explain that we have no idea how much is involved and we don't want to overcharge her. One way of handling it, I suppose, would be to place a piggy bank by the phone, but that's a bit crass. A meter would be much more to the point, and we have, belatedly, set the wheels in motion. In the meantime we have worked out an amicable compromise: one swift chat to Lisbon during the day equals a plate of green figs, peaches or tomatoes from Senhora V's garden. An evening call after 8 p.m. when the cheap rates start, is payable in beans, spinach or cauliflower according to season. This way everyone is happy—except the post office, who would rather be paid in cash.

If you decide you can live quite well without a telephone, it would be wise to make contact and a standing message-taking arrangement with the owner of the nearest one, in case of an emergency.

Other means of keeping in touch

If you decide to live in a truly rural area, warn your friends and relations not to waste their money sending you telegrams. These go to the nearest post office, where they can sit until the postman next makes his rounds. Which may well be twenty-four, forty-eight or, in the case of a bank holiday, at least seventy-two hours later.

From Portugal, it is much cheaper to make a quick overseas call from a public box than to send a telegram. Most have instructions in several languages, including English.

In 1978 we were surprised to find how many quite small organizations, and even private individuals, had invested in telex machines. Then we discovered just how long it took in those days to have a telephone installed and it all made much more sense. Telex machines are rented here, like phones, for a monthly charge of 11,150 escudos or about £53. The cost of installation is 35,000 escudos.

Finally there is Citizens' Band radio, legal in Portugal and quite widely used, particularly by taxi-drivers and boat-owners. If you are going to settle in a remote area, CB could prevent your being completely isolated, and you might even consider importing good-quality equipment with your household goods (see Chapter 7), providing you have owned it for at least a year. CB radio is licensed in Portugal. You get the necessary forms at the post office, and the annual fee was 500 escudos, the last time we enquired.

4. The Business of Buying

With prices rising all the time, it obviously makes sense to buy your Portuguese home as soon as possible. If you change your mind later on, and providing you have followed all the correct procedures, you should be able to re-sell quite profitably. And if you have elected to live in one of the popular holiday areas, your future home can almost certainly earn part of its keep through summer tourist rentals, until such time as you are ready to move into it.

There are, however, a couple of snags.

Under a new (1986) law, foreigners are not now allowed to buy more than 5,000 square metres of Portugal until they have been resident in this country for at least five years and have a Type "B" *Autorização de Residência* to prove it. The law also says that non-residents or residents holding a Type "A" *Residência*, the kind that has to be renewed every year, may only own one Portuguese property, be it a house, apartment or bit of land. See Chapter 9 about *Residências*.

There has been no change in the law about payments. Non-residents must still make their purchases in foreign currency, not escudos; and to do this, formal application has to be made to the Bank of Portugal for a licence to import sterling, US or Canadian dollars, Swiss francs or whatever.

These are the only restrictions on foreign ownership. But they do mean that you will have to wait until you are a well-established resident of Portugal before investing in a farm or a sizeable spread. And if you are buying ahead of time, be sure to buy in one of your names and not jointly. That way, both husband and wife can be property-owners if they wish, without contravening any regulations. Once you have your Type "B" *Residência*, you are treated like any Portuguese national and can buy whatever you please.

No matter where you choose to live in this country, the same laws and the same property-buying procedures apply. But you may find that the way in which those laws and procedures are administered vary slightly from district (*Conselho*) to district. Each one has its little idiosyncracies.

In the Algarve for example, where there is quite a severe housing shortage, in at least one *Conselho* it is a waste of time applying for permission to put up a pre-fabricated wooden house. The request is invariably turned down flat. But just a few kilometres down the road, the next-door *Conselho* sees nothing wrong with a pre-fab, providing all the other municipal requirements are met and the land on which the house is to sit has been approved for building purposes.

By now you must have some idea about where and how you want to live in Portugal. Do you plan to have a home by the sea? In a city, town or village? In a modern development or in splendid rural isolation? Are you thinking in terms of a compact apartment or a house with a garden? If you prefer a house, would you rather walk straight into one or buy a plot of land and build your own?

Finding an agent

Whatever the answers to these questions your first step is to find a reliable estate agent. Developments, of course, have their sales offices on site, but for any other kind of accommodation a good agent is your best bet because he or she can often offer much-needed help with the business of buying.

There is a local saying that every barman is a part-time estate agent in this area. Especially in the summer season. And you will undoubtedly hear stories about people who negotiated directly with kindly farmers and bought land for next to nothing. The stories may well be true, but they probably happened some years ago, when the property laws were a lot more lax and the people who were prepared to sell their land and houses were a lot less sophisticated. These days, unless you have made good and trustworthy friends in the area, you would be far wiser to deal through an agent. There is no shortage, particularly in the towns and the coastals resorts. The trick is to find a good one.

Though Portugal has an official Real Estate Association with headquarters in Lisbon and a code of ethics for its government-approved members, the organization is national only in name. The Algarve does not yet have a branch, which means that among the large number of honest, knowledgeable and very helpful agents you will also find a few cowboys, fly-by-night operators and agents that should not be touched with a ten-foot fishing rod. A look through the "Overseas Properties" columns of the British papers will tell you which agencies specialize in Portugal. You may even be lucky enough to find one who has gone to the trouble of producing an audio-visual presentation for prospective clients, starring properties in his particular area.

The Portuguese National Tourist Centre in London (New Bond Street House, 1–5 New Bond Street, W1) publishes a list of Portuguese agents, some of whom work closely with British ones.

A Portuguese agent should be licensed—and say so in his advertising. Study the advertisements in the English-language press, and ask everyone you know for advice. Recommendations and cautions, you'll find, are very freely given.

Legal help
Even with a well-recommended agent holding your hand, it is, to put it mildly, foolish to proceed with any purchase without legal help. Not because the vendor will try to rip you off but because the laws are complex and constantly changing, and because there is such an enormous amount of complicated paperwork involved.

This is not just a personal opinion. Not long ago, we were talking to the director of a large and well-known development and were amazed to hear how many people were apparently quite prepared to buy his expensive villas without any legal help. "Perfectly sensible people," he told us, more in sorrow than in anything else. "The sort of people who would never dream of buying so much as a pig-sty in England without their solicitor's advice. I think they must leave their brains at home when they come down here. I offer them our own legal services, or tell them where to find an independent lawyer if they prefer. But they don't want to know. All they want to do is pay their deposit and sign a contract."

You do not really need a Portuguese lawyer (*advogado*) to see you through the intricacies of property-buying—unless there is some irreconcilable dispute which looks as though it is going to end up in court A lawyer here is the equivalent of a barrister in Britain.

Normally, a *solicitador* can handle all the conveyancing, and his bill will be much more reasonable. If your estate agent cannot recommend one and the local grapevine is unfruitful, look in the Yellow Pages of the telephone book for solicitors in your area.

Then, too, there are a number of individuals and organizations who specialize in helping new and prospective residents. These are not necessarily legal practitioners, but they know the procedures backwards. Even more important, they know all the personalities and potential pitfalls at the local *Câmara* (Town Hall) and whether there are any bees in the municipal bonnet about pre-fabricated houses or anything else. Some of these invaluable people advertise in the English-language Press. Others are unearthed only by the standard procedure of asking around.

Even with an agent to help you find what you want, and someone to shepherd you through all the legalities, the purchase itself will take a minimum of three months. Very often, a great deal longer. So, unless you need an excuse to make several trips to Portugal, it may be better to give Power of Attorney to your solicitor or reasonable facsimile. That Power of Attorney, of course, applies only to this one specific transaction.

Buying procedures

You are still not convinced that you can't go it alone? Then let's look at the procedure for buying a simple piece of land.

Let us assume that you are going to build your own dream house. Touring around the countryside in search of *vende-se* (For Sale) signs, you have stumbled across the perfect spot: a tract of land with a well, electricity close by, good access and a sensational view. Remembering that as a non-resident you cannot own more than five thousand square metres, you have found all the stone markers with initials carved on them, paced the land and estimated that you are well within the limit. (Incidentally, there is no legal definition here of that useful word "approximately" in connection with land measurements. It is generally taken to mean ten per cent either way.) You have found the owner and, clutching your Portuguese dictionary, have managed to convey that you would be prepared to buy his land if the price is right. After a token haggle, a bargain is struck and everything in the garden looks lovely.

Now you must find out whether the land has been registered at the local tax office, the *Secção de Finanças*. Also if the owner has been granted building permission within the last year. If he looks blank when you ask these two questions, shake him warmly by the hand and go immediately for help—from someone who speaks Portuguese fluently and knows the Land Registry Office.

Land registration is not yet compulsory in Portugal—though the betting is that it very soon will be. If the field you have your eye on has not been registered, someone is going to have to delve through reams of records to establish that it does in fact belong to the person who is so happy to sell it to you.

When a Portuguese countryman dies intestate—and the majority do—land and other possessions go automatically to his immediate family. It might well be that the field where you want to build your dream-house is owned jointly by half a dozen people. If you are lucky, they will get together and agree that the only way to benefit from their inheritance is to sell the land and divide the proceeds. If not, you had better forget the whole thing and start looking elsewhere.

Building permission
In this case, let's say you have been lucky. The land has been properly registered and allocated its *artigo matricial* (file number). The owner is indeed the sole owner—but he has never applied for permission to build. So you must. And this is where the paper starts to build up—all in Portuguese, of course.

The first approval you need is from the *Direcção Regional de*

Agricultura, the Agricultural Department in your district capital: Faro, Beja, Évora, Portalegre, Setúbal, Lisbon, Santarém, Leiria, Castelo Branco, Coimbra, Guarda, Viseu, Aveiro, Oporto, Viana do Castelo, Braga, Vila Real or Bragança.

From the local Town Hall you get three copies of the map covering what you hope will be your land, and three copies of the area map on which that land appears, showing the roads and municipal boundaries. Outline your land in red on all six maps, and mark precisely where you propose to build your house, stating how many square metres it will occupy.

Send the map, with a letter in Portuguese requesting permission to build as indicated, and be prepared to wait at least six weeks for the Department's answer.

During this time, a representative will be sent to study the land. The records will then be checked to see whether it is designated for agricultural purposes or for building, or for both. Even though part of the land may have been earmarked for agriculture, if you have chosen a suitably rocky section on which to build, you will probably receive permission. And that does not mean you are obliged to farm the agricultural part. If the whole tract is designated agricultural, you are out of luck.

Armed with the Department's letter of approval, you must now make application to the local Town Hall (*Câmara*).

The *Câmara* requires yet another map showing the property outlined in red and the exact position of the proposed house, with its approximate area. Plus the reply that you received from the Department of Agriculture. Plus a formal letter of application in Portuguese stating what the building is to be used for. Since you are not yet a resident of Portugal, be sure to specify that you need this house for "a holiday home". As a resident, you would say you need it "for habitation".

After another inspection and unless the *Câmara* has any valid reason for refusing you, permission will be granted—with injunctions to comply with the local building regulations about style, use of a locally registered civil engineer and so on.

It is neither necessary nor advisable to part with the original copies of any documents. A notarized photocopy will serve perfectly well.

At this point, at least 2½ months after you started, you can now have the Promissory Contract (*Contrato Promessa*) drawn up by the vendor, your agent or legal adviser and registered with the official notary. Registration is not obligatory, you may be told. All the same, it is a sensible step. The contract, of course, is in Portuguese and you would be wise to have an exact English translation made for your own files.

The *Contrato Promessa* is a legally binding document which includes the description of the property as set out in the Inland Revenue records, its registration number, size, boundaries, the names of vendor and purchaser and the terms of payment. These are normally ten or twenty per cent of the agreed purchase price on the signing of this contract, and the balance on receipt of the Title Deeds (*Escritura*).

And here, as a non-resident, you find yourself in a Catch-22 situation.

Importing money

As already mentioned, the law says that foreigners living outside the country may buy Portuguese property only with foreign funds, and application must first be made to the Bank of Portugal for permission to import those funds. However, among all the bits of paper that the Bank requires in order to grant that licence is the Promissory Contract you have just signed—in exchange for the deposit in a foreign currency that you are not yet permitted to import.

Since it takes a month or more for the import licence to come through, the usual practice is to leave a sterling or other foreign currency cheque for the deposit with your legal adviser, who will cash it when the licence arrives.

Application to the Bank is made in triplicate and must be accompanied by a plan of the land and information on its size, the Promissory Contract, title of ownership from the vendor, permission to build from the local *Câmara* and a statement as to the nature of the building (holiday home or habitation). Plus, of course, notification of the amount you wish to import and in what currency.

As to that amount, it should cover the purchase price of course, plus legal fees, notarial fees (2% of the price), land registry fees (5%), *Sisa* or Property Transfer Tax (8–10% on land) and, if you are building immediately, the cost of construction. If you are buying now and building later, make a second application to the Bank when you need the funds.

There is no limit to the amount of money that may be imported and no reason, if the application is properly made, why you should not receive your licence (BAICP) quite quickly.

Now that Portugal is a member of the EEC, applications from nationals of other member countries are automatically approved, which is probably causing a great pile-up of paper at the Bank of Portugal. In pre-EEC days, you could expect to receive your BAICP within thirty days; now, you might well have to wait for three months before your application is processed. It is all a matter of luck.

A few years ago it was possible, though certainly not advisable, to save time by ignoring the rather tedious business of import licences. People who thought they knew better would bring their foreign currency in suitcases, make their payment in cash and congratulate themselves on saving a month or so of waiting. But they had forgotten one thing in their hurry. Without the BAICP to show the money had been properly imported into the country, there was no legal way in which they could sell their Portuguese property and take the proceeds out of the country. To apply for an Export Licence from the Bank of Portugal, you must produce the original BAICP.

But what happens if your situation changes in the meantime? You might decide, on reflection, to pay part of the money in sterling and part in Swiss francs, instead of the all-sterling payment you had originally specified. Or, instead of going through all the bother of building on that bit of land, you might suddenly want to buy an existing house in an entirely different part of Portugal. In either case or for any other reason, you must make an amendment to the application for an Import Licence, because funds must be used for the purpose stated in your application. If you change houses in mid-stream, you run the risk of having the funds frozen, which means interminable delays while the whole mess is sorted out.

Before the land is actually yours, you must pay the *Sisa*, the Property Transfer Tax. This is done by taking the Promissory Contract to the local tax office, and it may be a day or two

Living in the Algarve: a modern house in Vale do Lobo on the south coast, and (below) a country villa set amid orange groves

Decorative fretwork chimneys are the Algarve's trademark, and a reminder the Moors were here for five hundred years

In the street: Olhão is a prosperous fishing port with a strong North African flavour. (Below) The fish market

(Top left) Faro, the Algarve capital, was sacked by the Earl of
Essex in 1596 and twice devastated in the eighteenth century by
earthquakes (Opposite) The harbour
(Above) Fishing boats at Quarteira bearing the ancient
Phoenician decoration of the mystic eyeball

Modern terraced housing in the Algarve, and (below) a typical whitewashed cobbled street

Like every other
Portuguese city, Lisbon's
side streets are festooned
with fresh laundry

Cascais's pavements are
brightly patterned

Alexandre Eiffel designed the *Elevador* in Lisbon

before the transaction is completed.

The final step is the signing of the *Escritura* and the handing over of the Title Deeds. This is done by the *notário* who wants to see your copy of the Import Licence, your receipt of the *Sisa* payment and the Promissory Contract. All the details about the property, its vendor and purchaser are copied into the official book, which is then signed by both parties—or their representatives—and the land is at long last yours.

Ask the *notário*'s office for a copy of the *Escritura* and you will probably be told that it will take a few days to prepare, and it will cost roughly £4.

It is now your responsibility to see that the property is registered with the *Secção de Finanças*, so that they can levy the annual Property Tax, and with the *Conservatorio do Registo Predial* (Land Registry Office), where they will want to know whether this is a sole or joint ownership, if there is a mortgage or any other encumbrance on the land. All this information is contained in the *Escritura*.

It is, as you can see, quite a performance.

Time-savers
Unless you speak and write fluent Portuguese and have plenty of time to spend on the project, not to mention a saintly supply of patience, it is much easier for a non-resident to give Power of Attorney to a reliable and energetic local expert who knows the property-buying ropes. It is invariably quicker and usually cheaper in the long run.

However, if you still insist on being your own lawyer, there is one way you can save yourself a little time and very likely plenty of aggravation.

When you find the land or the house you want, make it a condition of buying that the vendor register it at the *Conservatorio do Registo Predial*, if this has not already been done. If there is any hassle about establishing ownership, he can deal with it.

And here is another hassle-saver. When you are looking for land on which to build, look for land that has already been built on. It does not matter how long ago the structure was put up or what state it is in now. If only the foundations are visible, that is fine. The fact that somebody once had a house there shows that it is not agricultural land, so there is no need to apply to the Department of Agriculture for permission to build.

With your Type "B" *Residência* (see Chapter 9) and the freedom to buy as much land as you want or can afford, you may find a tract that is big enough for two or three houses.

When you are applying for permission to build, apply at the same time for permission to build another house on that land. Should you ever want to sell off part of your property, it is a more attractive proposition if it is offered complete with permission. In some *Conselhos* you may run into complications if you want *artigos* for more than one other house —say, two or three. Some municipalities count three houses as a development (*urbanização*), and you then become involved in all kinds of expensive installations such as roads, street lamps and so on.

Buying a house

In many ways it is easier to buy an existing house, or even one that is still on the drawing-board, because someone else will have sorted out the question of land ownership. In the latter case, it will be owned and presumably registered in the name of the builder. Even so, it is always wise to check this out at the *Conservatorio do Registo Predial*, where the records are open for public inspection.

To draw up a Promissory Contract for the purchase of a house, the *notário* needs a copy of the Building Licence and Habitation Licence from the local *Câmara*. Or, if the house was registered before 1951, when these licences were invented, a certificate from the tax office.

When it comes time for the *Sisa*, the amount payable on a dwelling depends on its price and its use, and the tax operates on a sliding scale: from 10 per cent on houses costing less than 10 million escudos (£47,620 at the present rate of exchange) up to 17.5 per cent on anything costing more than 15 million escudos or £71,430.

But if the house is to be your first Portuguese home and your only home—if you have disposed of all your property in other countries (see Chapter 6)—then, providing you move into it within six months, you pay no *Sisa* on property costing less than 5 million escudos (£23,800). But you must not sell that home within six years of buying it. If you do, you then pay the *Sisa* that you previously dodged.

A *caveat*

If you are buying a yet-to-be-built house or apartment with payments to be spread over a period of time, there is one thing you should know.

There is a Portuguese law, designed originally to protect foreign investors, which says that if the buyer reneges on the contract, he loses his deposit and any other money he may have paid to the builder, or the vendor—who can often be the same man wearing different hats. However, if the builder/vendor breaks the long-term contract anywhere along the line, he is obliged to repay the buyer twice the amount that has so far been paid on the property.

All very right and proper, on the face of it, except that the law contains a giant economy-sized loophole which an unscrupulous builder can use to his advantage. This was especially true in the mid-1970s, when the post-Revolution dust had hardly settled and few foreigners were investing even holiday money in Portugal, let alone capital sums.

In those days, life was precarious for all Portuguese builders. Construction was at a standstill and, though nobody wanted anything built, employers could not legally let any of their workers go. Bricklayers, plasterers and all other tradesmen had to be fully paid for twiddling their thumbs. Not surprisingly, many small builders floundered and sank. But for the larcenous builder, especially in the resort areas, this well-intentioned law could be a life-saver, if he was prepared to gamble on the return of the tourist business. When tourism picked up, as it surely would, property values would rise—and fast. The apartment he could undertake to build for a ludicrous £6,000 or so in 1976 would almost certainly be worth three or four times that amount by 1980. With payments stretched over four years before the final Transfer of Title, there would be a small cash-flow and he could break the contract whenever he chose, with a little sleight-of-hand and for a maximum payment of £12,000; which, when the property was resold in a greatly improved market, left a substantial profit.

Today, with prices no longer rising so dramatically, there is not so much incentive for a double-dealing builder to snatch the property back from under your nose and leave you suddenly homeless. But it could still happen and, until this loopholed law is repealed, watch your step. And keep your ears open. If there is a local villain in your area who goes in for this sort of thing, you will very soon hear about him.

Don't, please, get the idea that the woods of Portugal are full of such brigands. The Portuguese are some of the most honest people on earth, and examples of this sort of skulduggery —along with gazumping and other well-known tricks of the property trade—are very rare. Though they may take time, the vast majority of property deals go through smoothly and cheerfully, with plenty of lasting goodwill on both sides.

Time is not, as you can see, of the essence in Portugal. But it very often is to the people who have made up their minds to move here. Not everyone wants to build his own dream house or even to wait around while it comes off the drawing-board. It is quicker and easier to spend that time hunting for something ready-made in the right price range.

Surveying

In Britain, and in most of Portugal, once you have found a suitable house, you have it professionally surveyed before making a final commitment. Not in the Algarve. Here, nobody seems to bother too much, and the only chartered surveyor we ever met spent most of his time at the nearby riding stables.

There is, of course, nothing to stop your having a survey carried out. A registered civil engineer will do it for you, but his bill will be quite hefty. Have the survey done in the winter, when any signs of dampness will be very apparent. During the long, hot Algarve summer, everything dries out, and any telltale marks can be effectively covered with a quick coat of paint.

Check that the house has enough circuits to support all the electricity you will be needing. Ideally, a three-bedroomed villa should have seven circuits, but a great many do not. If you decide a re-wiring job is necessary, you must first apply to the *Câmara* for permission to have the work done.

Since most Portuguese architects are men, and since very few Portuguese men would be caught dead in the kitchen, this is very often where you will find flaws in an otherwise beautifully designed house or apartment. Our own kitchen was obviously created for a left-handed midget with mole-like tendencies. The quite inadequate cupboards were all at ground level. Stove, sink and draining board were set in the most inconvenient places possible, and there was not enough space to open the oven door fully. The one accessible electrical outlet could only be used for blending, toasting or anything useful during daylight hours, otherwise it was needed for illumination. A two-way plug immediately blew the fuse. We did eventually find another outlet cunningly concealed inside a marble topped, tile-encrusted cupboard, and we are still debating whether it is worth ruining the very pretty tiles to get at it.

Portuguese kitchens, reasonably enough, are built to suit Portuguese cooks, which almost always means that the working surfaces are uncomfortably low for foreigners and often too low to accommodate standard British-made under-the-counter appliances such as dish-washers, freezers and fridges. Do some very careful measuring if you are thinking of bringing yours from Britain.

Management
When you have bought your Portuguese home, who is going to look after it until you are ready to move? Someone has to see that it is kept properly aired in between your visits, that the garden does not develop into a jungle and that all bills are promptly paid for water, electricity and taxes. You don't want to have to spend your holidays paying fines and trying to get everything reconnected.

One of the great advantages of buying into a development is that most of them provide this service—as well as dealing with all the paperwork involved in buying the property in the first place. Otherwise and unless you know someone who can be relied upon to make regular checks and deal with any crises, you might consider a professional property manager to keep an eye on things for you—for a fee. It is usually a good investment.

Property management is carried out on a contract basis, and fees will vary according to the area, the amount of work and whether your home is going to be rented or not. If you are planning to recoup some of your outlay through short-term holiday rentals, you would be very wise to have some responsible person in charge this end to supervise the day-to-day running, pay the maid and gardener as well as the bills, deal with any repairs and breakages and see that everything goes smoothly.

Some property managers combine the supervisory job with that of renting on your behalf. Others simply supervise and leave you to decide how best to fill your home with well-paying guests.

There are several ways of doing this, some more profitable than others. Again, the actual number of pounds or escudos you will put in your pocket depends very much on your area, the amenities you offer (a swimming pool in the garden increases rental values enormously), what you are paying for management, and how often and at what time of year you and your friends are going to use the place. If you insist on having your Portuguese holidays in the high summer season, you will naturally not do so well financially.

You can contract your home to a villa renting company and receive a lump sum for a given period without having to do anything more strenuous than sign the contract. You might make more money if you gave the rights to a rental company, or to several companies on an *ad hoc* basis. But then again, you might not. It depends on how heavily booked the house or apartment is.

The most profitable way is to do everything yourself, because you will have no commissions to pay. But it is very hard work, what with the advertising, the letter-writing, the phone calls and the business of trying to keep the bookings straight. Unless you are experienced in this sort of thing—don't.

We did it once and it was a nightmare. Though the house was booked solid, in season and out, once we had taken our clients' hard-earned money as a deposit, we felt totally responsible for the success of their holiday and, as the house was fifteen hundred miles away and without a telephone, we lived in a state of constant nail-biting anxiety in case something went wrong.

It is easier on both nails and nervous system to settle for a little less profit and hand holiday renting over to a professional.

Long-term rentals

Here you can run into problems.

Portuguese law bends over backwards to protect the tenant against landlords who try to turn him out or raise his rent unreasonably. Once a tenant has been in residence for a year, it can be incredibly difficult to regain possession of your home, no matter what the contract says. Even if he has defaulted on rent, sub-let without your permission, used the premises for unauthorized purposes or committed any other contractual sin, you still cannot throw him out. The matter has to go before the courts, and that can be a very, very lengthy business.

If you want to rent your home for a long period to anyone other than your nearest and dearest, you can get round this difficulty by having a contract drawn up for less than a year. It can then be renewed as necessary. Conversely, if you want to rent a house or apartment while you look around for or build your own home in Portugal, you may find it difficult in the Algarve. Many home-owners prefer to get their annual rent from summer holidaymakers and avoid any possible out-of-season difficulties. Some people we know rented their home to a family for eighteen months and, five years later, have still not managed to get them out.

In the Lisbon area and Oporto, where there is a large turnover of foreigners who come to work under contract, you are more likely to find accommodation for rent. And a high proportion of the advertisements stipulate that the premises may be leased only by foreigners.

The Portuguese do not bother very much about written agreements between landlord and tenant. But it is much wiser, as a foreigner, to have everything set down by a *solicitador* and then to have the contract endorsed and registered by a *notário*.

5. Bricks and Mortar

I don't know if it is the same in other parts of the country, but a great many people who come to live in the Algarve come with the idea of building their own house. Providing you can pop over to Portugal frequently to keep an eye on the progress, and providing you are in no great hurry, this is probably the way to achieve your ideal home.

As mentioned in the last chapter, it is always advisable to buy land with the help of a Portuguese expert. But once you get down to building, you need a fully qualified lawyer on hand, rather than a knowledgeable lay person, because you should have a contract drawn with the builder before a single brick is laid.

Life is, as you know, considerably easier if you have bought a piece of land that once had a dwelling on it—even if that building is now in ruins. Though the plans for your new house must be approved by the authorities, you are at least spared the boring business of first applying for permission to build.

It is sometimes possible to pick up a piece of land where building has been started but, for some reason, abandoned. In this case, those building plans have presumably been approved (your lawyer will check this out) and, in theory and unless you propose to tear it all down and start again, you are obliged to finish the building according to those approved plans. In practice, however, it is often possible to make interior alterations to suit your own requirements. But it is unwise to do this off your own bat. Consult with your *advogado* and with the architect you engage before changing anything.

Architects
Even if you are a qualified architect yourself, it is still necessary to work with a registered Portuguese practitioner. You can

certainly do all the designing yourself and produce the final drawings for presentation to the *Câmara*, but unless they are signed by a recognized Portuguese architect, they will most likely be rejected.

The key man is the architect. Once you have him lined up, he will probably be able to recommend an engineer and a firm of builders that he has worked with before.

How do you go about finding him? The same way as you go about finding anyone else in Portugal: talk to everyone in the area who has had a house built, study the English-language advertisements, ask your lawyer, talk to the people who run the developments round about. If you like the look of their villas, you might want to use their architect. If you don't, you know who to avoid.

There are companies in the Algarve—and probably in other provinces—who offer a complete package deal to people who want to build. They will find the land for you, have their own architects and engineers draw the plans, their own builders put up the house. Some will go even further and, once the house is completed, act as managers and rental agents until you are ready to move in. For many people, this is a splendid solution. Others wonder whether a company architect can devote as much time to their project as an architect who is directly employed.

If you can settle on an architect before you buy your land, so much the better. Let him look it over before you sign anything and, with his experienced eye and local knowledge, he may see something you have missed.

Conversions

This is particularly true where there is an old building on the site. Your original idea may have been to ignore or demolish the ramshackle structure after first checking to see whether you need official permission to do so. Your architect may look at it quite differently and see the nucleus of an attractive new home among the weathered tiles and bricks.

It is amazing what can be done with the smallest and most unlikely looking old Portuguese cottage—or what remains of one. Though the rooms are always too small for foreign comfort, they can be built around. Walls can be faced, strengthened or repaired. Old tiles, which are quite valuable these days, can be retained, while the roof is reinforced from inside.

One of the prettiest and most cleverly planned houses in this area started out a couple of hundred years ago as a miniscule two-roomed cottage with a spectacular view which the eighteenth-century owners probably never even noticed. The two tiny rooms are still there, intact but unrecognizable as one long living-room with a huge fireplace. The rest of the lovely, spacious house has been constructed around them, using materials of the same vintage.

It is not very likely, but if your architect cannot recommend a firm of builders, you will have to start asking around again.

Builders
Pay heed to the grapevine. As in any other business anywhere in the world, builders vary.

If we ever build our own house, we know exactly whom we would choose to do the job. We spent a large part of one summer hanging over the balcony watching a four-man crew construct a charming pair of duplex apartments across the lane. They did not move at any great speed, but every brick was laid with meticulous care and every phase was thoroughly checked by what we assumed was the company's clerk of works, who turned up at the end of every working day to take a look. As against that, we would run a mile from the firm that undertook to build a large and beautiful villa for a very well-known British theatrical couple. From all accounts and even allowing for the grapevine's tendency to exaggerate, nothing is going right, and the building process may easily outrun *The Mousetrap*.

Get quotations from three builders and have your lawyer prepare a contract with the one you finally choose. A local ex-pat ARIBA advises against the cost-plus system of payment. Better, he says, to tie your builder down to a completion date—and even to offer a handsome bonus if he keeps to that date. A bonus is probably a better incentive than the penalty clause which some people have written into the contract.

There will, of course, have to be an allowance for the constantly rising cost of labour and materials in Portugal. One way to keep this to a minimum is to insist that your builder procures all the necessary materials and has them on site before construction starts. All the materials, that is, except for cement, which deteriorates.

If you have been through all this in Britain, you might want to have the standard terms of the British contract incorporated into your Portuguese one. No honest builder will object to that, since the terms are fair to both sides. Write to the Royal Institute of British Architects (66 Portland Place, London W1) for a contract form, and ask your lawyer to interpret and incorporate it.

Building in Portugal is rather different from building in Britain. This is earthquake country, and therefore all structures have to be built so they could withstand a force of seven on the Richter scale.

Don't be alarmed and don't, for goodness sake, let this put you off the whole idea of living in Portugal. There are about one million earthquakes a year throughout the world—including several in Britain in recent years—and though we have felt the occasional tremor here in the Algarve, we experienced many much stronger ones in Quebec. All the same, it is nice to know that the Portuguese take sensible precautions, even though it does add to the cost of building.

Houses here have shallow foundations of rock, concrete and gravel, and the structure itself is supported by reinforced concrete beams or girders. The roof is supported by lintels of stressed steel beams. Walls simply fill in the spaces between the pillars and, since they do not need to be strong enough to hold up a roof, are usually made of hollow bricks. If there should be a tremor, the house is designed and built to ride it, and the roof remains intact.

In the Algarve, Portuguese houses never seem to have damp courses, presumably because everyone keeps saying that it is warm and sunny all year round in this province, and damp courses are therefore unnecessary. This is not strictly true. The Algarve can be exceedingly damp in winter, and though the Portuguese seem impervious to it, you would be advised to provide against damp, right at the outset. It is difficult, expensive and not wholly satisfactory to try to instal damp courses in completed buildings.

Design

Another thing about building in the Algarve: the authorities are quite fussy about the outward appearance of your house.

As you know, the Arab influence in this province is still very strong, more than seven hundred years after the Moors were finally driven out. Elderly Algarve ladies bundle themselves in voluminous black against the sun, just as Arab ladies do. Portuguese houses have small windows to keep the sun out, as Arab houses do. The whitewashed houses here, with their flat roofs and outside staircases, look very much like the houses in the Middle East—and the fishing town of Olhão, just east of Faro, could easily be mistaken for one in North Africa.

So don't be surprised if your architect's design features at least one ornate Algarve chimney—even if you are not intending to have a fireplace. Or a staircase leading to a rooftop patio. And if he puts the bedrooms on the ground floor and the living-room upstairs, so that the view is not wasted. This sort of thing is very much in keeping with the local style, which the authorities want to preserve.

People who have built here say that the more time you can spend with your architect, and the more information you can give him about the way you want to live, the more satisfactory your house will be.

A friendly and very talented builder says that the whole project starts long before you even find an architect: with a long, hard look at the way you want to live now and in the future.

Right now, he says, you may have a couple of children who are still small enough to share a bedroom. In a few years' time, they will want their own rooms. And perhaps their own bathroom. It is much easier and cheaper to build that extra room and bathroom now than to wait until they are needed, when you may have to do some conversion or add an extension to the house.

How do you feel about visitors? When you are ten or fifteen

years older, will you still enjoy having guests underfoot, or would a Granny Flat be a better arrangement? It is cheaper to build that extra accommodation now.

If you are a family of pack-rats, you will need plenty of storage space—something that often gets overlooked in Portuguese-built houses. If you are going to have animals around the house, a self-contained kitchen with a door that shuts dogs and cats firmly out might be more to the point than one of those jolly, open-style kitchens where the cook can do her stuff and still join in the living-room conversation.

Think hard, he says, about your present and future life-styles and, having done that, turn your attention to the fundamentals: the water supply, plumbing, electricity and heating.

Utilities
Water can be scarce in some part of Portugal and mains water a pipe-dream. If you have no mains, no well or underground water supply, you will have to have a *cisterna* built, which is quite a costly proposition. You will then have to arrange for water to be trucked in periodically to keep it filled. However, if city water does eventually come your way, you can always convert the *cisterna* into a swimming pool.

Even if you do have mains water, it is still a good idea to have an emergency water deposit for those times of shortage when the water is cut off. Since the four-year drought which came to such a devastating end in November 1983, causing enormous flood damage in the Lisbon-Estoril area, there has been a boom in the water-tank business, and containers are now being made in sizes that range from 125 to 1,000 litres.

We find that with a 250-litre tank on the roof we can manage quite nicely during our periodic water cuts, which inevitably happen in high summer when we have visitors. The cuts seldom last more than twenty-four hours, during which time baths are loudly discouraged.

The water in most of Portugal is extremely hard, which may be good for the teeth but which does not do much for pipes and water-heaters. They very quickly become thick with calcium deposit. Standard-sized water-softeners are available and simple to instal, and we were pleased to find that you can also get apartment-sized gadgets which fit neatly on the cold water supply pipe to the heater. Until we discovered this, our gas-fired heater was constantly being dismantled and sent away for a lime-removing acid bath.

Main drainage is non-existent in a number of areas, and if you have chosen one of them, you will have to make do with a septic tank. Get some good advice on the building of your tank. One or two in this village have obviously been poorly constructed, and the man who operates the local Sludgemobile keeps appearing to pump them out.

It is a good idea, our friendly builder says, to have individual stopcocks on everything that uses water: baths, basins, bidets, loos, sinks and outside taps. If a problem should crop up with any one of these, it can be rectified without having to shut the water off completely. I wish our not-so-friendly builder had thought of that.

Which reminds me, they don't seem to go in for U-bends here, and wash-basins appear to be held together with a small ring of transparent plastic and a single screw. Trying to unblock our bathroom basin one day, I undid the screw, and the basin promptly shifted four inches off its pedestal. We did get it together eventually, after some nasty outbursts of temper, and decided that any future unblocking would be done with either a plunger or a massive dose of caustic soda.

Electricity is another variable. Some parts of Portugal seem to have plenty, others do not. Even along the Algarve coast, which is one of the country's prime tourist areas, there are still great tracts of land without electricity—though it is officially scheduled for many of them. Now and again we come across a pile of concrete posts lying beside the road, a sure sign that something constructive is at least on the municipal agenda.

If you have electricity, you can find out from the *Câmara* about the local wattage or, if there is not a pole in sight, when you may expect to be electrified. How much it costs to be connected up to an electricity supply depends on whether that supply is owned by the municipality or by the national company, Electricidade de Portugal (EDP).

Speaking of electricity, it is as well to have your meters

conveniently placed outside the house, where they can be read at the appointed time, whether you are at home or not. This saves your having to read your own meter and fill in yet another form.

Plenty of Portuguese people manage quite nicely without any electricity. In the days when this really was an unspoilt fishing village and not a resort, the man who arranged for electricity to be brought in offered to connect up the local cottages for a ridiculously nominal charge—about £1, I believe. More than half the cottagers declined with thanks, and many of those have still not changed their minds. A number of foreign residents hereabouts also do without and seem content. Gas-powered appliances are available (see Chapter 7), and several people we know run their own generators.

One couple who are in the throes of building on a pretty piece of land miles from the nearest electricity pole are planning to make and put up a wind generator to provide themselves with free electricity. Other friends, who had been waiting years for the power lines to come their way, say it cost them between 1,500 and 1,800 escudos a month (£7 to £9 in 1985) to fire the generator that supplied their largish farm with electricity.

We are fortunate in having electricity in this village, erratic though it may be. But the monthly bills are large by Canadian standards and surprising by British ones. If your water is to be heated by electricity, consider having an automatic timer installed, so that you have hot water when you need it, but only when you need it, and your heater is not eating electricity twenty-four hours a day.

Keeping warm

Heating is a major consideration anywhere in Portugal and especially in the coastal regions. Coming from centrally heated, double-glazed Britain, you are going to feel the winter chills at first.

You will probably want to have a fireplace in the sitting-room, either a masonry model or one of the comparatively new (to this area) wood-burning stoves, which may not be quite so picturesque but which are extremely efficient. Talk very earnestly to your architect about an open fireplace, if that is what you have chosen. And try to have it constructed by someone who really knows what he is doing. A badly built fireplace is a pain in the neck—and we have the soot-blackened walls to prove it.

In the Algarve, where you will seldom see a fireplace in a Portuguese house, you can find out the hard way that the builder has ignored the tried-and-true rules about the proportions of fireplace and flue; and, very often, the one about the chimney being higher than the highest point of the roof. There is also a tendency to top the stack off with one of those decorative traditional Algarve chimneys that are frequently designed more for show than for blow—with not enough space between the elaborate latticework to let the smoke out.

If you are going to have a fireplace, have a good big one. The only available fuel is wood, which is comparatively inexpensive if you buy it and free if you scrump it from the countryside or the beach. Seventy pounds worth of hardwood logs lasted us right through the last unseasonably cold winter, with plenty to spare. When you are pondering a fireplace, consider the advantages of having it set higher than usual. Say, three feet or so off the ground, at bottom-warming level. Those three feet could be turned into a storage space where logs can dry out. Or, if the fire is set at ground level, storage niches could be built at the sides.

Your architect will make sure that the fireplace is properly positioned, so that more than one corner of one room is heated. On the other side of that warm wall there could be an equally warm bedroom, or an efficient airing cupboard.

Whoever was responsible for the fireplace in this flat obviously regarded it as a British eccentricity and stuck it against an outside wall in the corner of the sitting-room, well out of everyone's way. Not only is it impossible to arrange the furniture so that more than two people can toast, but half the precious heat is wasted. We must have the warmest balcony in the Algarve. Even so—and despite the fact that it smoked like a kipper factory until we had the insides torn out and rebuilt—we relish our fire. It has kept us and the apartment comfortably warm through this last unusually chilly winter at a fraction of the cost of gas or electric heating.

Do, please, make sure that yours really works properly before you move into the house. There is nothing more horrible than having to have it rebuilt, as we did, after you have settled in. We spent what went down in the family diary as Hell Week, picking our way through bricks and rubble, and an equally hellish fortnight afterwards removing dust from the most unlikely places.

However, if we had not lost our nerve, we could have got the apartment centrally heated while we were suffering Hell Week. Since the grate was to be demolished and rebuilt in the right proportions, our ingenious fire-doctor suggested that we could get more mileage from the fire. For quite a small sum, he said, he could fit radiators in the two other rooms and in the bathroom, to be fed by water heated from our new improved fireplace. He dazzled us with technicalities about wrap-around heat-exchangers and thermostatically controlled pumps, and for one mad moment it seemed a very attractive idea. The quite small sum turned out to be close to £700, not small enough for our bank balance. But it would, I imagine, be a lot less if the central heating idea was incorporated at building time, and we have filed it away in case we are ever lucky enough to build our own house.

Free heating

One thing we would insist on, if that happy day ever came, would be solar heating. It is the obvious answer in a country that has so much sunshine, and solar panels are beginning to pop up all over the Algarve. They are not very pretty, but then neither are the ubiquitous television aerials.

A solar system is quite costly to instal. However, the Portuguese government is so anxious to encourage energy conservation that it is offering long-term, low-interest loans to anyone who wants to have their water heated by the sun. Your architect will know all about this, where and how to apply for such a loan.

Our fire-doctor, who is also into solar heating, had another idea for us to consider before he put the fireplace back together again: to use fire-power as a cloudy-day back-up for solar-heated water. A very interesting thought, but it died on the vine when he admitted that the apartment would have to be repiped; and, though we could have got a government loan, we chickened out at the thought of all the upheaval.

But it is something to think about when you are planning to build.

A beady eye

Once building has started, try to come over to Portugal as often as possible to check on progress. Some builders in the south have a nasty habit of taking the crews off one project and putting them on another, if they think the client is not looking.

Do you know what to look for when you are inspecting a new building? We didn't, so we asked a well-known Algarve builder.

Think damp, he said. Make sure there are no ways in which water can seep into the house. Check, for example, that there are no cracks between the wall of the house and the surrounding terrace. Or between the tiles and the patio walls. Or between the roof tiles and the chimneys.

Flat roofs are not flat. They should slope imperceptibly from the centre so the rainwater can drain away. The same applies to balconies. Make sure that all flat roofs and balconies have enough drainage holes.

Aluminium window frames may not look so attractive, and they cost about twenty per cent more, but they are more practical than wooden ones, which may not be properly seasoned and therefore warp and fit badly.

Marble is one of the cheaper building materials here, and it is used lavishly. Splendidly luxurious in bathrooms and to a lesser degree in kitchens, where china and glass can easily get chipped, but lethal when it is used for outside steps. If you must have exterior marble steps or staircases, be sure the stone is not polished. When it becomes wet, marble is dangerously slippery.

Mildew on interior tiles, in bathrooms and kitchens, is not necessarily a sign that water is leaking into your house. It may simply indicate that those tiles have been stored outside while the house was being built—as you instructed.

The smell and feel of dampness in a new house may not be a sinister sign either. It could well be condensation. Fresh concrete, they say, can take about five years to sweat itself dry, during which time unsightly black marks can appear on the walls. To prevent this, make sure the builder applies a coat of damp-resistant exterior paint before doing the final outside painting.

Once again, look at that lacy Algarve chimney. And check the fireplace thoroughly. Not by stubbing a cigarette out in the grate, which we suspect was all that our builder did, but by building a good fire and then burning an oily rag on it.

Stupidly, we did not do that. Nor did we check the bathroom fittings very efficiently. With the first flush of the loo, ten litres of water torrented onto the floor, because we had not noticed that there was no connecting pipe between tank and bowl.

A habitable house

Officially, you may not move into your newly completed house until it has been inspected by the Provincial Architect and a representative from the local *Câmara*, and granted a Certificate of Habitation.

You'll notice that Portuguese countrypeople do not bother with such formalities. They will build one room of their house and move the family straight in, living there while they construct the rest of the house around themselves.

Don't be tempted to do this. As a foreigner, it is always better to do everything by the book—even though it is sometimes difficult to find out what the book says.

Even so, you can still run into problems, though they will not be of your making and nobody will be unduly cross. Between the time that your house plans were approved and the time the authorities have come to inspect the finished building, legislation could easily have been enacted that prevents the Certificate of Habitation being granted.

It happened in this apartment block, to the fury of the flat-owners who were waiting anxiously for the Title Deeds.

The builder actually made two stabs at getting the block certified. On his first visit, the Provincial Architect was peeved to find that some unauthorized alterations had been made and the exterior of the building did not look like the architect's elevations he had approved several years previously. Since the block was fully and illegally occupied by this time, partly by owners and partly by holidaymakers, there was a hurried discussion, after which it was decided that the plans would be redrawn to fit the building.

This, we were told, would take a month or two.

More than a year later the architect returned with the revised drawings. But, alas, the building was still not habitable. In the intervening months a new law had been passed which said that all bathrooms must have outside ventilation. Five of the eight in this building only had windows which opened onto landings, and they were not good enough.

We all settled down crossly for another lengthy wait. But two days later a couple of cheery workmen appeared to bore huge holes from the landings into the offending bathrooms, and to remove most of the landing windows. Nice and cool in the summer, but when the winter winds began we were all ventilated half to death.

However, the building was at last pronounced habitable, Title Deeds were exchanged and the permanent residents heaved sighs of relief.

Building costs
It can be a long and quite expensive business building your own house. Exactly how long and how expensive is difficult to say, for much depends on where you are planning to build and how relentless you are about cracking the whip.

A reputable builder in the mid-coastal section of the Algarve says he can do the job to your complete satisfaction within nine months, which is more or less the time it took to put up the duplexes we admired from our balcony.

As to the cost, in 1984 you would have expected to pay at least 30,000 escudos (£150) a square metre for anything built to an acceptable standard in the Algarve. Today it is more like

40,000 escudos (£190) and the old adage about getting what you pay for still applies.

On top of the bricks-and-mortar cost there is also the cost of the land, connection to utilities, taxes and architect's fees, which usually work out at around 2,000 escudos a square metre. For that, he supervises the job and pays the registered engineer who must, by law, be employed on any building project.

In other, less tourist-conscious areas, you may be able to get it all done more cheaply.

Your own electricity

Once the building is complete, whatever it is made of, pronounced habitable and registered in your name at both the *Câmara* and the *Registo Predial*, you then take your copy of the *Escritura* (Title Deeds) to the local office of Electricidade de Portugal to have the electricity supply transferred to your name and a meter installed.

There will, of course, be a certain amount of electricity flowing into the building before you do this, but only as much as is required for construction. And this is normally not nearly enough to run household gadgets without blowing fuses.

You are charged a monthly rental for the meter, and the price is based on the power the board is equipped to handle. The largest size costs around 1,000 escudos a month.

If, after you have been in residence for a couple of months, you still have not received an electricity bill, better check with the EDP office. You might have got lost in the shuffle of new customers, and you could well find that your electricity is cut off without warning because you did not pay the bill that nobody sent you.

Unlawful building

Do not even think about making any structural alterations, or adding any extras, after you have moved into your house without first finding out whether you need a licence to do so. The chances are you do. If, after a few months, you think it would be pleasant to have a swimming pool, you must first apply to the *Câmara* for a licence. It is a nuisance, but it is the law—and the law is now being more strictly enforced than it used to be.

Until 1983 many people, Portuguese and foreigners, looked at the modest price of a building licence and the fine that was levied if they were discovered building anything unlawfully. They calculated the licence-getting time (which is not really all that long) and decided the risk was worth taking. A very great deal of unlicensed building went on, and a great many fines were paid without a murmur.

Now the law has been equipped with pretty sharp teeth. The price of a licence has been increased, and the fine for unauthorized building is five times the licence price if the work is still in progress when the inspector comes round, ten times the licence price if the work has been completed. And that is not all. If they feel like it, the authorities can now move in and demolish that illegal building.

There is an immense fuss going on at this very minute about the impending demolition of a large colony of *clandestinos*, illegally built cottages on the islands off Faro and Olhão in the Algarve.

If you want to change anything more structural than a cupboard or build anything bigger than a dog-kennel in the garden, do find out first if you need a licence.

Prefabricated houses

It is not absolutely necessary to pay those formidable bricks-and-mortar construction costs, providing you don't mind being considered a little eccentric and getting bleak looks from friends in the construction business. After a few false starts, the idea of prefabricated Colt-type houses in either wooden or concrete panels is slowing gaining acceptance—even in the ultra-conservative Algarve.

When the first of the wooden prefabs appeared in the south in the early 1980s, people with housing problems were delighted. Here was a way to get all the space they needed at a marvellously affordable price, a mere fraction of the conventional building costs. They also liked the idea of being able to walk into a new house within weeks, rather than months. But not everybody was so enamoured of the unusual and un-

Algarvean log-cabin look and some local mayors vetoed wooden houses on sight.

The pioneering companies persisted, putting up show houses and engaging gung-ho salesmen who managed to collect a number of nibbles and down payments. Unfortunately, only a small handful of those first customers actually got their wooden houses built before the companies ran into difficulties, mostly financial, and one by one they folded their prefabs and silently stole away.

For several years after this fiasco, nothing much was heard about instant houses in the Algarve; though there were plenty to be seen around Lisbon and the north, in a variety of attractive designs. Then there was news that another Lisbon-based company had moved into the area, with a contract to build several dozen prefabs for one of the largest municipalities. These were the first of the concrete panel houses, more expensive than the wooden ones but still a lot less costly than bricks and mortar and with an acceptably Algarvean look to them. Interest in prefabs was promptly revived and a small complex of concrete houses was put up and completed by a local contractor at a nearby sports centre, where they sold like the proverbial hot cakes.

Whether they are made of wood or of concrete, the houses sit on a foundation of concrete and the price includes making and connecting up the septic tank, hooking up to water and electricity, all the tiling and carpeting and painting that is required.

6. Preparing to Make Your Move

Unless you are a complete gipsy and keep all your assets in a paper bag, you have some serious thinking to do if you are to leave the United Kingdom without handing the Inland Revenue people more than they deserve.

Some fifty years ago a British jurist said: "No man in this country is under the smallest obligation, moral or otherwise, to so arrange his affairs as to enable the Inland Revenue to put the largest possible shovel into his store."

Nobody is advocating tax-evasion, but it is your responsibility to make your affairs as shovel-proof as possible before you leave, with the help of your bank manager, your solicitor, stockbroker, accountant and anyone else who could count as a financial adviser. This may sound sneaky and un-British, but it is only common sense. It is also perfectly legal—and essential, if you want to protect your heirs.

Your problem with the Inland Revenue revolves around the question of your domicile, something that has apparently never been clearly defined in law. Since you have been living and paying tax in the United Kingdom you are, ipso facto, domiciled in the United Kingdom, and the tax authorities are reluctant to believe that you are about to forego all the benefits of British domicile to live in another country.

You can see their point. If they scratch you off the books without a struggle, you might come sneaking back—having removed your assets out of their reach—and it could be years before they caught up with you again. Until you have been officially established as "non resident and not ordinarily resident in the United Kingdom", they will keep tabs on you, maybe for as long as three years. And if you should die in the meantime, they can pounce on your estate and levy Capital Transfer Tax on all your assets, anywhere in the world.

So it is not enough to write a cheerful letter saying you are off to live in Portugal. You have to prove it.

It is actually much more of a palaver getting rid of your British domicile than acquiring your Portuguese one.

Changing your domicile

The fact that you can live in Portugal for 60 days on the strength of your British passport, and for another 180 days with a Residence Visa (see Chapter 9) is a start. But it does not really prove anything. Even when you have achieved a Type "B" *Residência*, with most of the rights of a Portuguese national, the Inland Revenue people know you can change your mind at any time and decide not to reside here any more.

You will have to do better than that.

A British chartered accountant who now lives in Portugal gives some very good advice to anyone trying to prove that they really mean it when they say they are leaving Britain to live abroad.

First, he says, get rid of any property you may own in the United Kingdom. The sale of your home is not subject to Capital Gains Tax, so that can be disposed of before you leave for Portugal, if it suits you.

Do not under any circumstances arrange to have any accommodation in Britain kept permanently for your private use. It would be nice to have a bed-sitter bolthole for holidays, but it is much more sensible to stay with family or friends, or to go to a hotel.

Write to everyone you can think of—friends, officials, tradespeople—telling them that you are leaving the country for good.

Resign from all your British clubs. You can always rejoin later, as an overseas member. And resign any directorships you may hold.

Buy property in Portugal, whether it is a house, an apartment or a bit of land.

Make a Portuguese Will (see Chapter 13) to cover your Portuguese assets such as property, cash and investments. Assets held out of Portugal should be dealt with in your British Will, which we'll discuss in a moment.

And although it sounds a trifle macabre and may even be gilding the lily a bit, he says that if you buy yourself a burial plot in Portugal, it would indicate to any interested observer that you really do intend to end your days in this country.

Finally, he advises Britons coming to live here to spend most of their time in Portugal, until their non-resident status is confirmed in the UK. Remember, you are still under surveillance, in a manner of speaking, and if you spend an undue amount of time gallivanting around Europe, the IR may wonder what you are playing at. One false move and you are back on their computer—if, indeed, you ever came off it.

It is particularly important to remember this when you are planning a return visit to Britain, which, of course, you are quite entitled to do—but you may only stay for a limited time.

As a non-resident of the UK, confirmed or not, you are now allowed to spend a total of only three months in that country during any one year. If you want to spend six months there without endangering your non-resident non-tax-paying status, you will have to skip the previous year's visit. Ninety days in one year, 180 days in two years—that is the rule. If you stay in Britain for one extra day, the IR has got you. They are adamant and utterly hard-hearted about this, and it is no use pleading illness as an excuse for outstaying your welcome. You should have taken a ferry to France and been ill there.

Having been so nasty about the Inland Revenue, I was surprised and pleased to learn only the other day, from an exceedingly well-informed gentleman who makes his living advising foreign residents in Portugal, that the IR people can be extremely helpful. He is in constant touch with the Foreign Dividends Department in Britain and says they give him excellent advice to pass on to his clients.

Protecting your assets
Now to the problem of removing your assets out of reach.

Consult your various financial advisers before you do anything. They will probably suggest that you sell those assets that are not subject to Capital Gains Tax: your house, your savings certificates, gilt-edged securities, cars and personal belongings up to the allowable limit.

If your stocks and shares are sold after you have left the country, they are also exempt from Capital Gains Tax. It is no use leaving them in Britain, because they will be taxed at source, even after you have officially been declared non-resident. Then you are faced with the tedious task of trying to retrieve that tax money from the British authorities.

While you are busily working to divest yourself of your British domicile, you are not, of course, a proper resident of Portugal—so what do you do with the money you have realized from your assets?

Until you are granted permanent residence in Portugal, you cannot open a proper Portuguese bank account, one that pays interest. All you are allowed is a Tourist Account, which has to be fed with foreign currency (no escudos) and which pays no interest. It is a useful account to have, if only to keep you going until your permanent residence in Portugal is established. As soon as that happens, funds from your Tourist Account can be transferred into a current or deposit account. But it obviously makes no sense to put large capital sums into it.

One answer is to keep money in the Channel Islands or some other offshore haven. The major British banks have branches in Jersey and Guernsey that specialize in expatriate business, and your bank manager or solicitor will advise you about this.

Don't forget, while you are involved in all this financial wizardry, that you are going to have expenses in both Britain and Portugal. Anything you leave in your British bank account is liable for tax, until such time as your status is settled. But as soon as you have a regular Portuguese account, it can be transferred here.

You will need to do some quite careful budgeting before you decide what money to put where. Remember, while you are struggling with figures, that your living expenses in Portugal are bound to be unusually high for the first year or two, while you are settling in. There are always unexpected expenses when you move house, and it does take time to learn how to live economically in a foreign country.

Also to be taken into account is the high rate of inflation in Portugal—coming down gradually, but still a great deal higher than the UK. If you are setting aside money to buy the furniture you saw on your last visit, set aside a little more than the price that was quoted then.

I don't remember going through all this when we first emigrated from Britain back in 1957. Of course, we had no assets, which probably explains it. As far as I know, we simply told the bank manager that we would pay off our overdraft from Canada, if that was all right with him. He then applied to the Bank of England for our External Account. Even so and after almost thirty years, we had to sign a Declaration of Residence only a few months ago and promise to tell the Inland Revenue if we ever thought of going back to live in Britain. These people never give up.

You will have to talk to your local Inspector of Taxes, naturally. There are forms to be filled and plenty of questions to be answered about when you are leaving for Portugal and what you are going to live on while you are here. If, after consulting all your experts, you still have some questions, the tax man will have the answers.

Pensions

With luck, all your queries will have been satisfactorily answered before you leave for Portugal. If not, write to the Inland Revenue Claims Branch, Magdalen House, Trinity Road, Bootle, Merseyside L69 9BB. Or, if you receive a pension or an allowance out of public funds, to the Inland Revenue (Public Departments) Foreign Section, Ty-Glas, Llanishen, Cardiff C54 5ZD. This address applies to people who have retired from the Civil Service or from one of the armed forces.

Now for the good news.

If you are drawing a retirement or a widow's pension, you will still get it when you come to live in Portugal. And if you are creeping up to but have not yet reached pensionable age and have been making your National Insurance contributions regularly, you can still qualify by continuing to make your payments from Portugal.

Have a word with the nearest office of the Department of Health and Social Security and they will explain about the various classifications and the amount of payment necessary to keep you eligible to collect at the age of sixty or sixty-five, as the case may be. The details are somewhat complicated, but you will probably be offered the choice of paying Class 2 (Self-Employed) or Class 3 (Voluntary) contributions. There will be a form to complete and send to the Department of Health and Social Security, Overseas Branch, Newcastle upon Tyne NE98 1YX.

Incidentally the easiest way to handle any remaining contributions you may have to make is to arrange for your British bank to send one annual payment to the Department. They will not be pleased to receive weekly donations in escudos.

War pensions, disability pensions and maternity grants are all payable at the full British rate. The widowed mother's allowance, too, is payable—providing the mother is living permanently in Portugal with the child. She will not, however, get any increase in benefit for the child.

Living in Portugal, it is difficult to keep pace with the changes in British law that affect pensions and other related matters. Such changes seldom make headlines on the BBC World Service, and after a while one tends to get tired of spending money on day-old British newspapers. It is all too easy to lose touch. One way to keep informed is to take out a subscription to *Resident Abroad*, a most useful magazine published by the *Financial Times*. It deals with local currency controls, offshore financial centres and funds, UK tax rules, pensions, investments and many other topics that affect expatriates. The address is Greystoke Place, Fetter Lane, London EC4 1ND and the last time I looked, the annual subscription was £17.50.

Legal and health matters
Now that your whole life is about to change drastically, your solicitor will almost certainly suggest that you take a look at your will and perhaps revise it. As mentioned, it is best to have two wills, one dealing with your possessions outside Portugal and another, in Portuguese, to cover anything you own in this country.

This is the time, too, to look into the question of private hospital insurance. You can, in theory, take yourself back to the UK for medical treatment under the National Health Scheme. But this is not always convenient or financially possible and though Portuguese medical charges are far from exorbitant, coverage is a good idea—if only for your peace of mind. If you already belong to BUPA or some similar organization, it is simply a matter of getting yourself reclassified as a resident abroad. If not, see pages 152 and 153.

Have a thorough medical check-up before you leave Britain and lay in a good supply of any prescribed medication. Have you managed to track down a local doctor in Portugal? Your British doctor will probably forward all your medical data to him.

If you have not yet found a medical man here, put that high on your list of things to do when you move to Portugal, or when you next come here on a fact-finding holiday.

It is a good idea to have a dental check-up too, and to get anything fixed that needs to be fixed. There are dentists in Portugal, of course, and good ones. But if you are moving to a fairly remote area, it may take some time to locate one.

Unloading

One of the most time-consuming pre-emigration tasks is deciding what you are going to bring to Portugal in the way of furniture and personal belongings (see Chapter 7). This is a two-part problem: first, what are you going to ship from Britain? And second, how are you going to dispose of the things that have to be abandoned?

If money is no object, you need not waste too much time on the second part. Just give everything away, to friends and to charitable organizations. But for most of us, the furniture that either won't fit or won't suit a Portuguese house represents a contribution—however small—to the considerable cost of moving. When you have distributed everything you are going to give away, the more time you can spend on disposing of the rest, the more profitable this whole dismal exercise will be.

We blew it completely when we moved, because we left ourselves no time to explore the various options. When we had finally stopped arguing about what we wanted to bring to

Portugal, all we could do was stage three weekend mini-sales that we advertised in the local paper.

What we should have done was talk to the specialists. A word with one of the city's auctioneers or a look through the sale rooms would have told us whether we had anything worth sending for sale by professionals.

We could also have studied the advertisements for Articles Wanted in all the local papers. People who take the trouble to advertise for specific items are usually prepared to pay more for them than people who come bargain-hunting. Some of the pictures that ended up in Portugal and have not yet emerged from their packing paper might have found homes in art shops or galleries. Quite a few of the books that we piled in the hallway and offered for a flat ten cents each would have fetched many times more if we had invited one of the several dealers in town to come and take first pick.

But all of this takes time, which was something we did not have. With more of it and some forethought, we should have been able to raise the cost of transporting our stuff from Canada to Portugal. As it was, our hurriedly planned jumble sales probably paid about one third of the cost—which was a great deal better than nothing.

The unobtainables

You will presumably have a fair idea by now of the way you will be living in Portugal and the things you will have to do without, either because they are too expensive in Portugal or because they are unobtainable.

Before we left Canada, we did remember to cancel all our subscriptions to magazines, papers and book clubs, realizing that the topical publications would be wildly out of date by the time they reached us, and doubting that we would be able to afford the books.

A few months ago, we learned that the American Book-of-the-Month Club has a special service for overseas members. You get the catalogue as usual, but you get no book until you actually order it. You are not burdened with and billed for books you don't want, because you neglected to cancel them in time. Whether any British book club has this service, I really don't know. But if you want to keep up with the latest publications, you could find out.

Alternatively, there are organizations in Britain such as the *Good Book Guide* (Braithwaite & Taylor Ltd., PO Box 400, Havelock Terrace, London SW8 4AU) which has a vast catalogue and will mail reading matter anywhere in the world at quite reasonable prices.

A perennial problem for those who settle here—or anywhere else outside Britain, for that matter—is the one about sending Christmas and birthday presents to the folks back home. Not only have you got to guess how long it may take a parcel to get from here to there, but there is always the risk that it may get seized by Customs and delayed while they make sure it contains nothing illegal. And it does spoil the fun of receiving a present when it is perfectly obvious from the green sticker that inside all that wrapping is a box of Algarve marzipan with a value of 350 escudos.

It is much easier to buy your presents in Britain. If you already know your Portuguese address, this is the time to write to your favourite shops—Harrods in London, Jenners in Edinburgh and so on—asking them to put your name on the mailing list for their Christmas catalogue. They will wrap your order and post it off in plenty of time. There are also organizations that make it their year-round business to solve expatriates' present-giving problems. H. L. Barnett (Brunswick House, Torridge Hill, Bideford, Devon), Grays of Worcester Ltd. (PO Box 45, Worcester WR4 9AD) and Egerton's (Axminster, Devon EX13 5DB) are three who produce useful annual catalogues.

In some parts of Portugal the local flower shops have never heard of telegraphing flowers to addresses in or out of Portugal. The only way we could send a bouquet to someone in Britain was through one of the aforementioned gift catalogues, until my husband had a chat with a florist in his home town one time when he was over in Britain. Now we simply send Mr Evans a cheque and he kindly delivers or Interfloras for us, which is just as quick and rather cheaper.

I am quite sure there must be florists in Lisbon and Oporto

who will wire flowers to other countries and I know there is an Interflora shop in Setúbal.

Talking of flowers and festive things, if you are coming to live in southern Portugal, you will have to start thinking about Christmas rather earlier than you did in Britain. We are not, thank heavens, subjected to the "Only so many shopping days" countdown or bombarded by hard-sell commercials for weeks, if not months beforehand. We nearly missed our first Algarvean Christmas altogether, with only one shop in the town specially decorated and no sign of cards on sale until it was too late to mail them out of the country.

Now there are cards around in shops and at the post office, in plenty of time for overseas mailing. And notices in supermarkets urging customers to order their turkeys. Do put your order in early. Last year, a friend of ours left his order until Christmas Eve and all he could get was a hen bird that was not only alive and well, but the mother of chicks. The turkey family became pets and our friends had a vegetarian Christmas.

Timing

One more thing to add to your Check-Before-Leaving list: The date of your planned arrival in Portugal. We were so anxious to get to our new home that we even managed to arrive on the wrong day.

There are, as you know, a great many holidays of one sort or another in Portugal: official bank holidays, Roman Catholic holidays, purely local holidays when everything shuts and the townspeople go off to celebrate their local saint, not to mention those unofficial occasions like the four frentic days of the pre-Lenten Carnival, and the neighbourhood summer *Festas* when everyone is out enjoying themselves.

On page 220 there is a list of the twelve Bank Holidays and the Church Festivals, which are more piously observed in the north than they are in the south. It would be as well not to arrive in Portugal on any of these days. We arrived on one of the *Feriados Obrigatórios*, after travelling for forty-eight hours, to find the town shut tighter than the proverbial clam and no one around to sell us even a loaf of bread.

No driving licence?

Finally—and this will probably not apply to more than a small handful of people—in Chapter 9 you will see how simple it is to exchange your British driver's licence for a Portuguese one. But what about those who do not yet hold a licence and who, knowing how long it can take to get one in Britain, have wild ideas about applying for their first one in Portugal?

Forget it.

Forget it, that is, unless you are confident and bilingual enough to take both the written and actual driving tests in Portuguese, then to go through the lengthy business of medical tests and pounds of paper, also in Portuguese. By the time you have had a couple of the obligatory driving lessons—on the "wrong" side of the road, through an unfamiliar town, on a busy market day—you will be a gibbering wreck.

Get your licence before you come to Portugal.

We were talking about this not long ago with a British travel courier who needed a driving licence before she came to work in Portugal. But in her particular town the waiting list for the test was so long that she would be nowhere near the top of it by the time she had to leave Britain for her new job.

If you need a licence in a hurry, she told us, the place to get one is Malta. Providing you have done a little L-plate driving and are not a complete beginner, you can take the required number of lessons from an English-speaking instructor, pass your test, collect your licence and still have time left over on a two-week package tour to lie in the Maltese sun. This, admittedly, is hearsay. But the source is reliable, and if you are faced with this problem, it would be worth checking it out.

7. What Are You Going to Bring from Britain?

If you're smart, as little as possible.

Firstly, because it costs a great deal of money these days to haul your furniture and personal belongings from Britain through France and Spain to Portugal. And the cost per cubic foot, about £2 at the moment, is not likely to go down.

Secondly, because you can now buy just about everything you need to furnish a home, right here in Portugal. Maybe not in your nearest town, but certainly in the capital and in the larger cities. Even in the Algarve, which has always lagged slightly behind the times.

Thirdly, it is quite possible that some of the furniture you love dearly and which looks so perfect in your present home will not suit your new one. And there are probably things that you have used and enjoyed for years in Britain that are quite useless in Portugal. Like the water-powered dish-washer we dragged across the Atlantic, not realizing how precious and often scarce water is in this particular area. And the vast copper preserving pan which would hardly fit in the Portuguese kitchen, never mind on the stove.

As I've said, this reluctance to get rid of things was one of our biggest and costliest mistakes. If we had taken more time to consider and been more realistic about the things we could live without, we would not have spent so many months wondering why we could not get the contents of a three-storey house into a two-bedroomed flat.

We did have a small excuse. In 1978 it was very hard to find attractive flat-sized furniture in the Algarve. In the few furniture shops at our end of the coast almost everything we saw was huge and hideous. Or, if we did stumble over anything we liked, it was expensive by Canadian standards.

Had we cased the area properly instead of larking about and

enjoying our Algarve holidays before we moved here, we would have known that we stood a better chance of finding what we needed in the foothills town of Loulé, rather than in the coastal shops. We would also have asked more people where to buy what.

The most successful movers we have so far met brought absolutely nothing from Britain, except their clothes and their very personal belongings. They arrived with suitcases and stayed in a series of furnished villas while they searched for and found every item in their very attractive apartment.

Electrical goods

We did know before we moved that in those days electrical goods of all kinds were scarce and very expensive. Armed with a supply of adaptors, we brought the small, indispensable kitchen gadgets—mixer, toaster, slow cooker—that worked reasonably well, when we had any electricity. They were something of a sensation in 1978. Our old toaster-oven, common enough in Canada, was much admired here. Now you can buy the latest models in the next village, at quite sensible prices.

Nobody in their right minds, not even us, would seriously consider shipping large electrical appliances across the Atlantic. But quite a few people bring refrigerators, freezers, washing machines and dish-washers from Britain.

If you are planning to do the same, check first that the appliances you want to fit neatly under your kitchen counter do in fact fit. As already mentioned, Portuguese counters are lower, because Portuguese cooks are lower. Also check carefully in your area to see about servicing the appliances you are going to bring.

Seeing the reassuring name Hoover all over our local town, we acquired a small British-made Hoover washing machine. But it did not care for the erratic electricity supply in this village, and the motor died within a very few months. Had we done our homework properly, we would have known that this particular model was not available in Portugal and that a replacement motor would have to be imported from Britain. When it eventually arrived, it cost rather more than the whole machine and did not last much longer than the original motor.

If you are coming to live somewhere slightly rural, where the electricity supply fluctuates, a stabilizer might be a good investment. They cost quite a bit in Portugal and are probably not all that cheap in Britain. But current that is constantly going up and down does nothing for a refrigerator, washing machine or electric typewriter, and a good stabilizer should help prolong the life of these and other costly machines.

Electrical goods are much more plentiful now, but heavily taxed and still expensive. If you see something you need, buy it on the spot because prices can shoot up almost overnight. The Moulinex food-processor I seized on for what my sister said was a remarkable £33 was priced at more than £50 two weeks later.

Moulinex, Hoover, Philips and several other familiar names may not have service facilities in your immediate area, but they do have them in Lisbon, which is the next best thing. A look through the Lisbon phone directory (available in post offices that are large enough to sport public telephones) will tell you all. If you do not find the name you want in Lisbon, try the Oporto directory. If there is no help there, leave whatever it is in Britain.

If you are thinking of bringing a typewriter, and in particular an electric typewriter, you should certainly investigate the service facilities. The two most widely used machines in Portugal are Olivetti and Olympia, and there should be no trouble getting either of those fixed. But for almost six years now, it has been impossible to get spare parts for Smith-Corona machines, even in Lisbon.

You can buy the very latest in electronic typewriters here, at a price. And there is an extra charge of almost £40 to get the keyboard changed over from a European arrangement to an English one.

It is possible that you have chosen to live in a region where there is not yet any electricity. That will at least cut down on the decision-making.

You will find piped gas only in Lisbon and in one or two of the larger Algarve developments. Everywhere else it comes in large, small and camper-sized canisters of either butane or propane gas.

Even if they have electricity, most people cook with gas because it is less expensive. Water can be heated with either gas or electricity, and there are gas-powered refrigerators and irons on the market. If you are shopping around here for a gas cooker, there are some excellent European models available, but look carefully at the oven regulator. Not all of them have numbered markings.

What about furniture?

This is such a personal matter that I would not presume to give any advice. Only you know what you want to live with. But I would remind you of the high cost of haulage from Britain to Portugal—more than £10 for something the size of a tea-chest, £60-plus for a single wardrobe—and suggest that you look very carefully at those leather-upholstered armchairs and decide if they will fit well into a small apartment, or if they will swamp it.

Remember, too, that you can now buy very attractive and functional furniture here, if you look around.

The mahogany, chestnut and cedarwood furniture made in the north of Portugal is traditionally large, heavy and ornate. Beautiful, often, but generally more suitable for spacious country houses than for small villas or flats. In 1978 we had quite a lengthy and frustrating search for beds that were not elaborately carved and decorated with simpering cherubs. Now you can find anything you want, including space-savers like sofa-beds, beds that pull out of cupboards and ones that fold up neatly to make daytime chairs.

Nowadays, Portuguese-made furniture can be as modern and streamlined as any other. Stylish, too, and by no means expensive.

Don't bother to bring your patio furniture. You can buy beautiful outdoor tables, chairs and sun-loungers here at very reasonable prices. Or, if you are building your Portuguese home in the sun, you could consider having tiled seats and tables built at the same time, around the pool or on your terrace. You see quite a lot of bench-type seats built right into the walls and then tiled, which are very attractive and practical.

If we were moving to Portugal now and doing it more intelligently than we did in 1978, we would not bring one stick of dining-room furniture. Nor the upholstered sofa and chairs. And certainly not the large and, as it turned out, quite unsuitable high-pile carpet that we thought would help keep the apartment warm in winter. It did, to give the wretched thing its due. But if you live within walking distance of a beach, that kind of carpet becomes immediately filled with irremovable sand.

Nor would we bring any but the most precious pieces of glass and china. And only half the kitchen equipment that came with us in 1978. No, make that a quarter.

People who plan to rent their Portuguese home to holiday-makers for a season or two before coming to live here usually find it easier to equip their flat or villa completely with Portuguese-made items. As you will see in a minute, foreigners emigrating to Portugal are allowed one duty-free consignment of furniture, and most people want to save this privilege for their own belongings and not those that are going to be used by tourists.

Furnishing for rental usually means furnishing for summer rental, and this, as you know from your own holidays here, can be quite simple. People who come here for the sun and the beaches do not expect to find a houseful of antiques and sterling silver. By the same token, though, they do expect a reasonable standard of comfort for their money and are not amused to be fobbed off with garden furniture in the living-room, camp beds and a candle stuck in a wine-bottle to show they are on holiday.

If your plans include a spell of interim renting, you would be advised to talk to an expert specializing in contract furniture. There are plenty of them around, and they know where to buy everything that is needed, and at the best prices. If you are buying into a development, the management will very likely be able to handle this for you.

At the moment it costs approximately £5,000 to furnish and equip a three-bedroomed, two-bathroomed villa for summer guests, and about £3,000 to fit out a two-bedroomed, one-bathroom apartment. For these prices, says the director of one of the most popular Algarve developments, you should be able to provide everything your tenants require.

We might not bring as much furniture if we had to emigrate all over again, but we would still bring the same large collection of books—horribly expensive to transport, but worth it if you are lost without something to read. English-language books, like so many other things, are more easily available these days, but the grottiest paperback is still too costly for comfort.

On the subject of books: do include some up-to-date reference material when you are packing yours. You never know when it might come in useful. A first-aid manual, do-it-yourself books, medical information for both humans and animals.

Bring, too, the essential ingredients for a well-stocked medicine cupboard. Bandages, dressings and other things you may need to cope with minor accidents; the pain-killers and analgesic ointments you are accustomed to; lotions and potions to deal with upset stomachs, flu bugs and whatever is likely to ail you during the first few months.

All these things are, of course, easily available in Portugal and you can buy some quite surprising medicines over the counter without a prescription, but the brand names and the manufacturers' names may be different and, until you find your way round the chemists' shelves, there is a certain security in being medically self-sufficient. If you are felled by gyppy tummy almost before you have unpacked, it is easier to reach for the trusty Enterosan than to travel to the nearest Portuguese chemist to explain what you need.

The clothes you bring will naturally depend on where you have chosen to live.

You are unlikely to need a ballgown or tails in the depths of Beira Alta, but you might very well need some formal clothes in Oporto and almost certainly in Lisbon, Estoril and Cascais. The Algarve is, on the whole, fairly informal, but there are still a few functions where everyone dresses up, to a greater or lesser extent, especially around Christmas time and the New Year.

Don't discard all your British winter clothing. Although Portugal is technically a southern country with a sub-tropical climate and the Algarve is promoted as being warm all year round, it can still get surprisingly chilly, especially on the coast. Damp, too. Bring a warm winter coat. We are glad of ours maybe two or three times a winter, and if you find you don't need yours in Portugal, you will certainly need it if you make a winter trip back to Britain. Think twice about bringing a valuable fur coat, though. There have been a couple of days when one would have been nice, even in the south—and several more days, I daresay, in the north. But you may have a hard time finding summer storage facilities, except in David Kit's excellent establishment in Lisbon.

Clothes are a little cheaper here than they are in Britain, and you can buy good-quality garments without any difficulty in Lisbon and the larger towns. Boutiques abound and get better every year, and there are also plenty of talented dressmakers around and tailors who will turn out slacks and shirts—not necessarily at Hong Kong speed, but at very modest prices.

Boots and shoes are, as you know, among the really excellent bargains in Portugal. The leather is beautiful, the craftsmanship is fine and the prices are a fraction of those in Britain and North America, whether you want high-fashion footwear or farming boots.

As you can see, there is plenty to think about before you start calling the moving men. Take your time over it, and take a good look at what is currently available in Portugal before finally making up your mind what to bring. Top-of-the-head decisions are not always the best ones, and second thoughts can sometimes be expensive.

Importing your belongings

Under the present Portuguese law, if you have been granted residence in this country (see Chapter 9) or if you hold title to unfurnished property in Portugal, you are allowed to import duty-free whatever you like in the way of furniture and personal possessions—providing that everything you bring has been yours for at least one year and, if necessary, you can prove it.

You are afforded this privilege just once—as a family—and your duty-free consignment must arrive within three months of the date of the granting of your residence or from the signing of the *Escritura*, the transfer of Title Deeds. Husband and wife may not make individual applications for this duty-free importation, and if, at any time after those three months, you suddenly remember a whatnot you wish you had brought with you, you will need plenty of money and even more patience if it is to join you in Portugal.

It can take up to a year to get an import licence, starting with your application to the local office of the *Ministro de Finanças*, and the duty you will be asked to pay will be enormous.

There are six handsome bookcases either lurking in the Lisbon Customs house or being enjoyed by someone who bought them at auction, that arrived long after the rest of our furniture. In fact, we had almost given up hope of ever seeing them again when a terse Portuguese note from the *Alfândega* informed us that they were awaiting collection from Customs. Splendid. They also informed us that the duty would be £1,000, more than three times the original cost. Not so splendid. The correspondence went on for months, with letters from us, from solicitors, from shipping agents, with photocopies of dated sales slips and anything else we could think of, but to no avail. In the end we decided to cut our losses and save our stamps. The Customs, we said, could either keep the bookcases or send them back where they came from. I hope they found a good home.

Before you do anything, do please check with the nearest Portuguese Consulate to make sure there have been no recent changes in this one-off duty-free importation of household goods. It is unlikely, but the ground-rules can change so suddenly in Portugal that it is always better to check everything.

The whole business of getting your belongings from there to here is, as you can imagine, fraught with paper.

Once you have decided what you want to bring, everything —down to the last teaspoon—must be itemized, and the list then translated into Portuguese. If you are lucky and they are not too busy, the Portuguese Consulate may do this for you. If not, they will tell you where to take your list for translation in triplicate. When this has been done, you have to sign a Declaration of Ownership, and you will then, after a small pause, be issued with a Certificate of Baggage from the Consulate, which remains valid for ninety days.

Unless you live within easy distance of a Consulate, you can spend days—not to mention pounds—travelling to and fro with passports and bits of paper. Remembering too late that you should have included the serial numbers of everything electrical on your inventory; or, if you are bringing your British television set, that you have to produce your current TV licence.

Luckily for you, if you are coming from Britain, it is not necessary to go through all this time-consuming, nerve-shredding performance unless you want to. There are a number of reputable long-distance moving companies, including one that specializes in transporting households to the Algarve, and they will look after all the paperwork—for a fee of £45.

Pay it and be thankful.

In Canada there was no such service, because we were going in the wrong direction. Even the Consulate officials were stunned to hear that we wanted to move to Portugal; they spent their days dealing with people who had just come from Portugal or were trying to arrange a relative's westward passage to Canada. As for the Canadian shipping company, accustomed to moving people west or south from Montreal, they hardly knew where Portugal was.

The people who move you
Choose your moving company carefully and, if you think it will help, ask the British residents in your part of Portugal who they used. If their movers were good, they will be glad to tell you about them.

Ideally, you need a company that uses road-trains, which are great pantechnicons equipped with sleeping-quarters for the crew. The men who pack up your house in Britain will put each piece in place in Portugal, and they will never have let your belongings out of their sight during the whole long trip.

Look for a company that has warehousing facilities at this

end. You may wish to send your furniture on ahead. Or there may be an unexpected hitch in your arrangements—your newly built house may not be quite ready, or if you are taking over existing accommodation, the occupants may not be able to move out on the agreed date. If your moving company has no Portuguese warehouse, you will have to chase around looking for storage space.

You also need a firm that has a fleet of smaller moving vehicles in Portugal. There are any number of town and village roads that have difficulty in accommodating two donkeys side by side, never mind a house-sized pantechnicon.

One more advantage in dealing with a specialist company: they will deal with the Customs going through Europe and when they finally reach Portugal. Once you have waved the van off from your front door in Britain, you do not have to give it another thought until you supervise the unloading in your new Portuguese home.

Most companies offer a free estimate of the cost, and you will probably want to have two or three quotations before making your choice. Beware of an outfit whose prices are surprisingly low, and never accept a quotation made over the phone. Everything should be down in writing—including a guarantee that, if anything goes wrong with the original arrangements, your move will be completed at no extra charge.

Compared to transporting your possessions by sea, road haulage is a breeze.

If, for some reason, you must import by sea, do choose a company that goes in for containers. At least we had the good sense to do that. Our belongings were sealed into a box on the Montreal docks and only unsealed when they finally reached Lisbon, long after the promised date. We were duly notified by the company's agent in the capital, along with what we thought was a pretty casual request that we post him our passports and a blank *Papel Selado* neatly signed in the middle.

Since we were both brought up to believe that a British passport was more precious than gold and you never, ever let it out of your sight without an argument (except, reluctantly, when staying in a European hotel), we were appalled at the very idea. As for signing a blank and official bit of paper that somebody else was going to fill in with heaven knows what while we weren't looking—what kind of a country was this?

It was all very alarming, but that's the way it was done in 1978. With the gravest misgivings and because we were not keen to go to Lisbon ourselves, we did as we were asked. Our passports were returned in short order and, within a matter of days, our belongings arrived at the apartment.

Nowadays, you'll be glad to hear, most shipping companies have local agents and there is seldom any need to post anything. The agent simply takes the passport and does the necessary.

And the fiscal-stamped *Papel Selado* disappeared in 1986, thank heavens. But everything official is still written or typed on special blue paper, *Papel Vinte-e-Cinco Linhas* (Twenty-Five Line Paper) which is readily available at almost any stationery shop and costs seven escudos a sheet.

Importing pets

One of Portugal's biggest attractions, as far as we were concerned, was that we could bring our zoo. So can you.

They will not be able to go back to Britain, of course, without spending the mandatory six months in quarantine, but there are no quarantine restrictions here. If you yourself want to return for a holiday, there are good boarding-kennels and plenty of friendly people only too happy to dog- or cat-sit.

There is very little fuss about domestic animals, but a certain amount of paper is involved. Your dog or cat must have a certificate of good health from your local vet, and an export Certificate from the Ministry of Agriculture, Fisheries and Food (Hook Rise, Tolworth, Surbiton, Surrey). Also veterinary certificates to show that the animals have valid inoculations against rabies and distemper. Take all these papers and have them officially stamped by the Portuguese Consulate.

Regulations say that incoming animals must be inspected by a Portuguese veterinarian at the point of entry into Portugal. If you are planning to drive here with the livestock, ask the Consulate about arranging for a vet to be at the border crossing when you enter the country from Spain.

Airlines all seem to have different ideas and rules about

flying animals, and some are a lot kinder than others. If you are proposing to fly with your pets, do a bit of shopping around. Some airlines insist that even a chihuahua must travel in the freight compartment; others will allow up to two small dogs or cats in the passenger cabin, providing the flight captain approves and providing the animals travel in secure boxes. Unaccompanied animals go in with the freight, which is a horrifying thought on a seven-hour transatlantic flight, but no big deal coming from Britain. A matched pair of Norfolk terriers recently arrived in this village and, apart from being a bit bewildered, suffered no ill-effects at all.

Your own vet will advise you about the wisdom of administering a mild tranquillizer, and what to do about feeding, watering and walking an animal prior to its flight.

The type of carrier is important to the animal's comfort. See if you can find one that is not made of mesh but is more solid and with plenty of ventilation holes. We managed to fit ours out with some magnificent boxes made of heavy-duty board with domed clear plastic lids, so they could see out if they wanted to and curious passengers could not stick their fingers into the boxes. Much better than steel mesh because, if an animal becomes frightened during the journey, it can injure itself badly by clawing to get out.

A travelling box should be large enough for the dog or cat or whatever to stand in it when it is closed, and it is advisable to buy the container well ahead of flight-time and leave it nonchalantly around the house, so the animal can get used to it.

On arrival at either an airport or a border-crossing, the animal and its documents will be looked at by the Portuguese vet, who will give you yet another piece of paper. When you get to your final destination, this should be sent at once to the Department of Agriculture in your provincial capital (look under *Direcção Regional de Agricultura* in the phone book for the address).

"Some time during the next two weeks," the lady vet at Lisbon Airport told us in May 1978, "a veterinarian will call on you to examine your animals and make sure that they are still in good health.

We wished it had been as easy to get ourselves to Portugal.

8. Wheels Within Wheels

People who are deeply attached to their cars are not going to be pleased with the Portuguese regulations.

Simply stated, the law says that a permanent resident in this country, whether foreign or Portuguese, may not drive a foreign-registered car. And that is that. Only tourists and temporary residents, those who have been granted a Residence Visa but have not yet got their *Autorização de Residência* (see Chapter 9) may drive a car with foreign plates, and then only for six months. After that, the car must be taken out of the country or imported permanently—and expensively.

If you don't feel too strongly about your present vehicle, you have no problem. Everyone, including the people at the British Embassy in Lisbon, will unhesitatingly advise you to sell your car before leaving Britain and buy a Portuguese one when you get here.

Cars are costly in Portugal, if you want anything more exciting than a small Mini-type runabout. A new MG Metro Turbo was listed at £5,000 in September 1986, an Austin 1.3-litre Maestro at £6,000 and a Rover 216 at almost £10,000. And that, if you're going a little white around the gills, was after the government had slashed the sales tax on cars quite dramatically, from 35 to 25 per cent.

British Leyland and Renault are now the only manufacturers of small cars that have assembly plants in Portugal. But no more Minis are made here. All that BL put together are their Mini-Mokes, which were listed last September at just over £3,250 or much the same price as a Citroen Club or Mehari Plage.

If you refuse to part with your precious Porsche, prepare yourself for the long and quite costly business of importing it and having it re-registered and equipped with Portuguese plates so that it may be legally driven.

The British Embassy advises that you start this protracted procedure good and early. It can take months to complete and sometimes as long as a year. And six months after you receive your *Residência*, you can be in trouble if you're found still driving around with GB or other foreign plates.

We had some British neighbours who became entangled in automotive red tape, poor things, on account of their British-registered Volvo and their reluctance to ask anyone for advice. After living here for almost a year as temporary residents, which was and still is legal, both husband and wife applied for their *Residências*. In due course these arrived and they went merrily off on the next stage of the paper-chasing exercise, to see about getting their Portuguese identity cards. On their way to the British Consulate they were flagged down by the police on one of the routine summertime road-checks. These, as you probably know, are nothing to get excited about as long as you are carrying all the necessary documentation. In the normal course of events, unless you are driving a stolen car or one that is obviously unroadworthy, or you have the car laden with something suspicious, you are delayed only as long as it takes the *Guarda* to check your papers against the car registration.

In this case, seeing the British plates and taking it for granted that our neighbours were tourists, the police asked for the car papers and the driver's passport. Had they done what they were asked, they would have been waved on their way with a friendly salute. But unfortunately, instead of producing the one passport, they both brandished their nice new *Residências*, delighted to show them off. But in those days there was no such thing as a six-month grace period. If you had a *Residência* in your hand, it was illegal to drive with foreign plates.

In the height of the summer and with other more serious things on their minds, the Algarve traffic police seldom go looking for this sort of trouble. But with the evidence shoved up their noses, these had no alternative but to take names and addresses and to set the official wheels in motion. Two days later our local lawman came plodding up the hill with the news that the unmatriculated Volvo was grounded until such time as it was properly imported and registered. And so was our neighbours' equally GB-ed caravan. He was sorry, but there it was. Their names were now on the blotter, and there was not a thing he could do about it.

So the Volvo sat outside the apartment block gathering dust, and the caravan sat on the campsite doing the same, while their unlucky owners spent more than six months bussing and training themselves to the provincial capital and up to Lisbon, talking to Customs officials, solicitors, the British Embassy and the Portuguese Automobile Association.

To add to their troubles, Murphy's Law—"Anything that can go wrong will go wrong"—was operating at full strength. Essential papers got lost, co-operative officials or those who could speak some English suddenly got transferred to the other end of the country, whole files mysteriously disappeared for weeks on end. Every time we asked how the battle was going, it seemed as though some new disaster had struck.

In these circumstances even the most level-headed person could become quite paranoid, convinced they were being deliberately persecuted. They were not, of course. The whole horrible shambles was conducted with the greatest kindliness and patience on the part of the authorities, in spite of the language difficulties. But once those official wheels had started to turn, there was no stopping them until the matter was settled.

In the end it cost close to the new-car price to import and matriculate the Volvo, and another hefty sum to legalize the caravan. Plus a lifetime supply of aggravation and a considerable amount of hard cash for coffee, to entertain the constant parade of policemen who appeared at their door with many apologies and more paper.

When they were at last allowed to move the car, to the relief of one and all, they drove into town and promptly collected a parking ticket.

If, after that horror story, you still propose to import your car, consult the various British automobile clubs: the AA, RAC, RSAC. They should be able to give useful advice on the most up-to-date regulations. You could also ask their professional opinion about obtaining an EFTA or EEC certificate;

some people say it is a good idea and will save a few pounds, others think it a waste of time.

Talk, too, to the Portuguese Consulate, and if you want to contact the Automóvel Clube de Portugal, their address is Rua Rosa Araújo 24, 1200 Lisboa.

Import duties are now based on the type of car, the size of engine and the vehicle's age. The total cost can be anything from 40 to 150 per cent of a figure that is determined by the Portuguese Customs, plus the Portuguese equivalent of VAT at 16 per cent, plus all sorts of other fees and extras. Right now, 1987, it would probably cost about £720 to import a small ten-year-old car. There is no point in going too deeply into this because the rules are about to change once again. All I can say is, do check very carefully with all the experts you can find, before deciding to import your car.

The business of matriculation, re-registering the car and getting Portuguese plates is very expensive and exceedingly tedious, and it can easily take a year to get everything in order. But until it is in order, you cannot get comprehensive insurance coverage for your car.

Matriculation begins at the British Consulate, with a Consular certificate and the notarizing of your papers, which are then handed over to a Customs broker who will take it from there.

Spares and servicing

Whether you are bringing your car or buying one here, do look carefully into the question of servicing and availability of spare-parts.

Around Lisbon, Setúbal and Oporto you are quite likely to find specialists to handle the more exotic makes. In the Algarve it might be more difficult. In the hinterland, it is unlikely. For the latest information on who fixes what and where, consult the current red Michelin guide. It lists the specialist garages in various Portuguese towns and cities.

Another consideration is the local terrain. In the Algarve, for example, the main east-west road that runs parallel to the coast is currently being widened, modernized and generally improved out of all recognition. Further inland, there are some perfectly acceptable paved roads, a great many rock-strewn perpendicular tracks and a plethora of pot-holes. For country-dwellers who can afford it, this is Range Rover country.

Buying a car in Portugal

At the moment, diesel fuel is cheaper than either Normal or Super petrol. It might therefore be worth considering the purchase of a diesel-fuelled car if you are going to do a great deal of driving. The 1986 price of a Peugeot 504 Diesel was £2,000 over the list price of the petrol-driven model.

Another thing. If you are in the market for anything other than a regular people-carrying car—a Land Rover, say, or a van—take great care about its registration. Portuguese categories can vary a great deal and, though the dealer will take care of the paperwork, make sure he knows exactly what you want to use the vehicle for—business or pleasure or both. If your new Hiace has been inadvertently registered as *tipo mercadorias* or *serviço vendas*, both of which are strictly commercial categories, you are not allowed to take more than three people in the cabin.

Check the original proposal carefully and insist on a written guarantee of the *livrete*, the registration book. If wires get crossed and an error is made, never mind whose fault it is, re-registration can be costly.

Buying a new car in Portugal is much the same as buying a new car anywhere else. You decide what you want, order it and then wait. Then wait some more for the extras you ordered with the car and which did not arrive.

Make sure the dealer understands that you want the manufacturer's manual in English.

Second-hand cars

Don't, please, have any grandiose ideas about bringing your car from Britain and selling it in Portugal before the six months temporary duty-free period is up. Granted, secondhand cars fetch an enormous price in Portugal—anything up to four times the going rate in Britain—but for reasons that are now obvious, no Portuguese resident is much interested in buying a right-hand drive car with foreign plates.

There is no great difficulty in buying a secondhand car here, except for the size of the cheque you will have to write. You can expect to pay around £1,500 for a car that the MOT would consider roadworthy. The universal caveats about secondhand car buying apply as much in Portugal as they do anywhere else.

There are dealers in most large towns, and used cars are advertised in the *Anglo-Portuguese News* and on notices stuck up in supermarkets and restaurants, and they are also broadcast on the local grapevine.

Taxes

With the ever-rising cost of petrol—111 escudos a litre for Normal in early 1987 and 115 escudos for Super—driving is becoming an expensive pastime in Portugal. But taxation, by British standards, is a bargain.

The older your car and the smaller its horsepower, the less you pay. This year, we'll pay £3 for our nine-year-old made-in-Portugal Mini. For a new medium-sized vehicle, the tax in 1987 will be about £12.

Start watching out for notices about road tax payments in May. Sometimes things get delayed and in 1986 it was July before we were able to get our new sticker from the tax office.

The documents you take to pay your *Imposto Sobre Veículos* are the ones the police want to see when they wave you down in a road-check:

1. The *livrete*, the small green card gives car details and is issued by the Ministry of Transport and Communications in Lisbon.

2. *Titulo de Registo de Propriedade* issued by the Ministry of Justice, which identifies you as the owner of the car described in the *livrete*.

3. The current year's receipt from your insurance company showing that you carry the now mandatory third-party coverage (see Chapter 11).

4. The receipt for last year's *Imposto Sobre Veículos*.

Plus, naturally, your valid driving licence, which, if you are a bona fide resident with an *Autorização de Residência*, must be a Portuguese licence (see Chapter 9). If you do not yet have a

Residência, you show your British or International Driving Licence.

Driving in Portugal

Always carry your documents when you drive and, until you receive your *Residência*, your passport. If you are driving on a Portuguese licence outside this country, you will need an International Driving Permit from the Automóvel Clube de Portugal and a Green Card from your insurance company, or from any border point.

From time to time, new regulations about cars are promulgated and promoted on Portuguese television and in the Press.

Seat-belts have been compulsory for several years now, and if a driver or a front-seat passenger is spotted unbuckled, they can be fined on the spot—and quite heavily. More recently, wing-mirrors and rear-wheel mud-flaps were declared essential equipment on all cars, and right-hand wing-mirrors on vans.

At the moment, and not before time, great attention is being paid to the problem of drinkers who drive and vice versa. The breathalyser made its Portuguese début towards the end of 1983, and the figures for those who failed the test that first Christmas were frightening.

The legal alcoholic limit started off at 0.8 per cent, which everyone thought bad enough. It has recently been reduced. If you are stopped, tested and found to have more than 0.5 per cent of alcohol in your bloodstream, you can spend the night in the slammer. Severely impaired drivers will stay there until a doctor pronounces them sober, be heavily fined and have their licence removed for anything up to a year.

There is a rumour going around that the limit may even be reduced again, and taxi-drivers are rubbing their hands in anticipation.

If you have driven in Portugal while on holiday here, you will know the local hazards. If not, take care and don't let your insurance lapse. Without wishing to be rude to our hosts, it is fair to say that outside Lisbon and Oporto the standard of driving is not always of the highest.

It is understandable, when you think about it. Before 1974 very few Portuguese people owned cars. Now a great many do, and the country is full of first-generation drivers. Before the Revolution, friends tell us, you would probably not meet a dozen cars on the road from the Algarve up to Lisbon, and an approaching vehicle was such a novelty that waves and hello-there toots were always exchanged.

One thing we noticed, coming from a large North American city: though the Portuguese drivers were naturally not as expert as the Canadians, who can take their tests on their sixteenth birthday, they are incomparably more courteous. Even in Lisbon, which is thick with traffic, nobody leans on their horn if you are a split-second late starting up on a green light. If you get muddled in the maze of one-way streets, which is all too easy, other drivers do not lean out of their windows and yell insults, as they are apt to in Montreal. In Lisbon they toot, beam and make incomprehensible signals to indicate that something is wrong. They will even stop to let you into a lane of traffic, which amazed us.

Here in this holiday area, where the roads become solid with summer traffic and you can easily sit for forty-five minutes in the blazing sun waiting to cross Portimão bridge, the Portuguese drivers are patient and philosophical about it all. If you hear an angry *obligato* on a horn, you know without looking that it is a tourist.

Traffic keeps to the right, as it does on the rest of the Continent, with overtaking on the left and traffic coming from the right having priority at junctions and intersections of equally important roads. The standard international road signs are used in Portugal. It is illegal here to:

1. Drive with full headlights on in built-up areas.
2. Have small children or dogs in the front seats.
3. Drive, as already mentioned, without the seat-belts buckled.
4. Carry a spare can of petrol in the car.

Keep an eye on the petrol gauge, especially on long journeys, because filling stations are rather sparse. There are none, for example, on the forty-kilometre stretch of road between Lagos and Sagres in the Algarve—a busy road in summertime. And if you run out of petrol while you are crossing Ponte do 25 de Abril into or out of Lisbon, you will definitely be in the doghouse. You must keep close to the right-hand side of the bridge and sit there, waving a white handkerchief out of the window until help arrives. If you have broken down, you will be towed away without reprimand. But if you have merely run out of petrol, you will be fined and obliged to buy ten litres of juice from the bridge authorities, to teach you to be more careful in future.

The speed limits for cars and motor-cycles are 60 k.p.h. in built-up areas, unless otherwise posted, 90 k.p.h. on ordinary roads and 120 k.p.h. (74 m.p.h.) on highways. There is also a highway minimum speed of 40 k.p.h. For cars towing trailers, the maximum speeds are lower: 50 k.p.h. in built-up areas, 70 on ordinary roads and 80 k.p.h. on the highways.

City parking is difficult in summer but almost a pleasure in the winter, when there are not too many tourists, at least in the south. Though there are municipal car-parks (ours charges 12 pence to look after your car, all day if you want), street parking is permitted, except where specifically forbidden by the sign with the red diagonal slash and also by bus stops (*paragem*), where a section of the curb is marked with hard-to-distinguish yellow lines.

So far, nobody has introduced parking meters, meter-maids and all those other urban nasties, but this is probably too good to last.

If you are unlucky enough to collect a parking ticket, take no notice of the people who tell you confidently that you can pay the fine at any police station. It's a myth. In this area, at any rate. The local police were not remotely interested in accepting the 400 escudo fine we incurred one day at the other end of the Algarve and, to avoid wasting an entire day and half a tankful of expensive petrol, we had to beg an east-bound friend to settle the matter for us.

Local hazards

Night-driving can be a little hairy, especially in the country-side, where unlit donkey carts amble along the roads and pedestrians are invariably dressed in black, which makes it impossible to see them until it is almost too late. Dogs, cats, rabbits and hedgehogs come hurtling out of the bushes and under the wheels, obviously miscalculating the speed of these new-fangled machines after generations spent dodging the slow-moving donkey carts.

Not all Portuguese drivers have quite got the hang of headlight-dipping, and in the Algarve you will also meet on-coming tourists who have staggered off the plane and into their rented cars, setting off from the airport before they have discovered the right switch.

Motorbikes can be a menace at any time, day or night. I don't know how it is in the north of Portugal, but in the south they are notorious for their habit of coming up on the right side of a car, which is unnerving.

Other daytime dangers to watch out for are the flocks of sheep and goats spread all over the road, maverick cows that have escaped their hobbles, small children and grown-up passengers alighting from country buses and marching across the road without a look to see if there is anything coming. Not forgetting the tourist in the unfamiliar rental car who suddenly stops without warning to ask the way. And the local driver who does the same thing to have a chat with a perambulating chum.

Keep a good safe distance between you and the vehicle in front of you, and be agreeably surprised if you get any warning of its intention to turn or stop.

Be particularly wary of lorries piled high with oranges, tomatoes, potatoes, beer crates or any other cargo that can slip its moorings and cascade all over the road.

The accident rate in Portugal is very, very high.

Help!

Fortunately, the highways at least are well furnished with emergency telephones which are connected to the nearest police station.

So far, we have had only one occasion to use an SOS box, when we were flagged down by a group of motor-biking youths, one of whose number had had what looked like a quite nasty accident. Being somewhat the worse for *vinho*, his friends tried to stuff the unfortunate lad into our Mini—and only stopped trying to bend him and insert him in the back of a two-door car when we finally persuaded them that it would be better to call for professional help.

To ring for help, whether you need the police or an ambulance, you simply press the SOS box button and state where the accident has occurred. Or, if you don't know where you are, give the number written on the front of the SOS box. Mercifully, it doesn't much matter if the person who answers speaks no English. The Portuguese and English words for 'police' and 'ambulance' sound much the same in an emergency: *policia* and *ambulância*.

The Portuguese have a gruesome curiosity about accidents and, if one happens, a crowd will gather in seconds, even if the road was empty when the trouble occurred.

Only a few years ago it was considered extremely callous and ill-mannered for a passing motorist to drive on past an accident—even if he had obviously slowed down and looked to see if there was anything he could do to help. The crowd could get quite upset, and the departing car be followed by angry shouts of disapproval. That has now changed. The crowds still come out of the woodwork to stand and stare and discuss the matter, but someone has usually run to the nearest SOS box or telephone to summon assistance. If you can establish that fact, there will be no hard feelings if you drive on about your business.

If you happen to be first on the scene and if you find a telephone before you find an SOS box, dial 115—the all-Portugal number for any kind of emergency.

Every car in Portugal should carry a red emergency-warning triangle. Should you be involved in an accident or have a breakdown on the road, set the plastic triangle out about a hundred metres behind your car, to warn oncoming traffic that you are in difficulties.

Incidentally, it is seldom the slightest use appealing to your regular filling station—or any other filling station, for that matter—for help with mechanical problems, however slight. Most of them can do very little more than fill your car with petrol, oil, water and air, clean your windscreen and, *in extremis*, give you an encouraging push to get you started. Things mechanical usually have to be handled either by the specialist garage that deals with your make of car or by a freelance car mechanic in the area.

After all this, you may very well decide that you can manage very nicely without a car. Plenty of people do, using public transport with, perhaps, a rented or borrowed car for a special excursion.

If someone offers to lend you their car, ask if they will also give you a signed declaration that you are driving with their permission and their documents. It would be embarrassing, to say the least, if you were stopped in a routine road-check and nabbed for car-theft.

9. The Great Portuguese Paperchase

Since this is a Latin country, there is a great deal of paper in Portugal. And a great deal of one's time in the early days can be spent trundling from one office to another in search of the requisite bits of paper that will result in one or other of the various cards that must be carried, not only by foreigners, but by everyone in Portugal.

It's no wonder that European men tote those dinky little handbags.

Be prepared to chase around. That is, unless you can find a reliable individual or service that specializes in this sort of thing and who will do all the forthcoming donkeywork for you. There are such people (scour the advertisements and ask around), and their fees may seem high, but if you need your documents in a hurry, or if you have followed some poor advice and become enmeshed in red tape, the money is well spent.

You will very likely get some bad advice. Take no notice of the character you meet in a bar or on a golf course who tells you that you don't need one particular piece of paper or that he knows a short cut. If you are coming to live in Portugal, you must be properly documented, and the procedure for acquiring your official resident's permit, your fiscal number, identity card and driving licence is clearly laid down.

If you try to buck the system by, for example, applying for your Portuguese driving licence before your identity card, you will get nowhere. And it is no good grumbling about the system. This is the Portuguese way, and since you are going to be a guest in this country, you will have to adapt to it.

You start on your paperchase before you leave Britain, if you are going to buy property in Portugal.

Your fiscal number

Anyone in this country, resident or tourist, who wants to buy a house, an apartment, a bit of land or even a car must have a fiscal number, which appears on a small card known as a *Cartão de Contribuinte*. If you are buying into a development or through an estate agent, someone from the office will escort you to the *Secção de Finanças*, the tax office in the nearest town, to help you get your number.

There is nothing to it. You produce your passport, if you are here on holiday, and are given a simple form to complete in duplicate. One copy of the form is yours, and your temporary fiscal number is shown in Section I, at the top right-hand corner.

Don't waste time trying to memorize it. In due course you will receive your permanent card from Lisbon, and it will have an entirely different number. This is the one that appears on a variety of documents: tax returns, for example, if you pay tax in Portugal (see Chapter 12), and papers that have to do with the buying and selling of anything more substantial than a push-bike, or with any business dealings you may subsequently have in Portugal.

Now for the serious stuff.

Residence Visa

This should not be confused with a Tourist Visa, which the citizens of some countries require before they can even holiday here. As a British national you do not need one of those, as you know, and you can enjoy Portugal for sixty days on the strength of your passport alone. But once you decide to live permanently in Portugal and for several months before you actually plan to move, the paperchase begins in earnest—with your application to the nearest Portuguese Consulate in Britain for permission to reside in Portugal for sixty days.

The authorities, reasonably enough, will want to know something about you before they grant that permission. So, at the same time as you ask for the application forms, write to someone you know who is already resident in Portugal and ask if you may use their name as a reference. Your sponsor can be Portuguese or a foreign resident, but he or she should be someone of certain standing in their community and a person you know fairly well. In due course, they will receive a note requesting their presence at the local police station, where they will answer questions about you and your family. (Until last year, a van-load of police used to turn up at the sponsor's door, which was somewhat unnerving.) But the reference will be followed up, you can bet on it. And your request to be allowed to live in this country may be granted or rejected on the answers the police receive from you and your friends, and on their own conclusions. So choose your sponsors with the greatest care.

While you are waiting for the application forms to arrive, get passport photographs taken—even if your current passport is still valid. Your mug-shot appears on several of the documents you carry around, a number of photographs are kept on various files and, one way and another, you are going to need at least eighteen pictures for official purposes.

By the time you read this, there may be several more reasons why you need to supply one, two or three photographs, so you might just as well order a couple of dozen prints and be done with it. And two of those prints must be in colour. A new law has just been passed insisting on colour pictures for identity cards (see page 129)—which probably means we will all have to get new photographs and new cards, curse it.

And there is one other thing to be settled before you start filling in forms. Do you know where your parents were born?

If you don't, you had better find out now, even if it means a trip to Somerset House. Because you are going to be asked this question any number of times once you get to Portugal. It crops up on just about every bit of official Portuguese paper including those that appear when you have even the smallest of dealings with the local police. Not that the authorities here are particularly interested in the answer, because as foreign residents we are all quite easily identified. But in a country where every third person seems to have the same surname, and where you could probably turn up half a dozen António José Oliveiras in any sizeable community, for the locals it is a different matter. The authorities want to be sure they are talking to or about the right António José Oliveira—the son of

António Filipe Duarte Oliveira who was born in Sintra, and of Maria Manuela Simões Oliveira, born in Setúbal.

When the applications arrive, complete them as directed and return them to the Consulate with three photographs of each applicant and a letter from your bank manager stating that you have enough money to support yourselves for those sixty days. The fact that you will almost certainly be granted a Residence Visa does not entitle you to take a job in Portugal (see Chapter 10), but if your bank manager considers that you can live on your available money, that is all the Portuguese want to know. They are not interested in your bank balance or where the money comes from, just so long as there is enough to keep you going.

It can take anything up to six months for your application to be processed and it will cost you the sterling equivalent of 2,500 escudos. If Lisbon approves of the answers you and your sponsors have given, your Residence Visa will be granted and your passport stamped to that effect.

You now have ninety days in which to move yourself and your family to Portugal.

When your Residence Visa expires, sixty days after your arrival in Portugal, it can be renewed for a further two months. Take your passport to the nearest office of the *Serviço de Estrangeiros*, the Portuguese Immigration authorities, with evidence that you can support yourself for another sixty days. You can take 30,000 escudos in cash or a copy of your Tourist Account statement. Your passport will be restamped and your stay extended. You may do this twice, allowing you a total of six months in Portugal as a temporary resident.

Strictly speaking, if you have not decided by this time that you really do want to spend the rest of your days in Portugal and have applied for an authorization to do so, you can be asked to make up your mind one way or the other. But in fact this seldom happens. As things stand at the moment, you can probably go on living here on this exceedingly temporary basis for years. But you must leave the country every sixty days, if only for an hour or two.

In the Algarve people drive or take the train to Vila Real de Santo António, ferry across the river to Ayamonte in

Spain and have their passports duly stamped on re-entry to Portugal.

Applications for a Residence Visa cannot be made in Portugal. If you are here as a tourist and decide you want to stay for ever, you will have to go either back to Britain to apply for the Visa or to the nearest Portuguese Consulate, which will be in Spain.

Permanent residence

When you have finally decided that you really do want to live permanently in Portugal, you must apply for your Type "A" *Autorização de Residência*, the red-and-green card bearing your photograph, signature and/or thumbprint.

This is the first step in your quest to acquire all the privileges of a Portuguese national—except, for obvious reasons, the right to vote in a Portuguese election—and it is valid for one year. Applications from upright British citizens are seldom refused. But a Briton who has been foolish enough to run foul of the police or who has blotted his copybook in some way may have a problem.

At this stage, the Type "A" *Residência* is the most important of the several documents you will collect, for without it you cannot get your Portuguese driving licence or your very useful identity card. Nor can you even think about going into business here. This is how you go about it.

Take your passport to the nearest British Consulate (see page 235) where, incidentally, you should register your presence and make sure your address is noted. In exchange for 1,080 escudos you will get a consular certificate stating that you are indeed a British citizen and that you have no criminal record.

Next stop is the local office of the *Serviço de Estrangeiros*. Take with you the consular certificate, your passport, three black-and-white photographs and a sheet of the blue paper ruled with twenty-five lines (see page 109) and 2,500 escudos. You will not be required to write anything on the paper or to fill in any forms. That is all done for you and all you have to do is pay over the money and return in person to the office in two weeks' time. Your *Residência* has to be signed in front of an official before you can tuck it away in your wallet, and you should carry it with you at all times.

Carry all your papers with you at all times. You can be arrested if you fail to do so, we have just discovered. It is very unlikely. But if you happened to be in a bar, say, when the police came in looking for someone in particular, everyone present would be asked to show their papers, and it could be awkward for you if you had left yours at home.

With your *Autorização de Residência* you will also get a typewritten note informing you of your obligations as a resident of Portugal. They are not unduly taxing.

You are asked to observe the laws of the country scrupulously. To inform the *Serviço de Estrangeiros* within eight days if you change your address. Also to inform them beforehand if you are proposing to be out of the country for more than ninety days. Finally, to make sure your authorization is presented for renewal in one year's time, between the dates mentioned in the note. It seems very little to ask in exchange for permission to live in this delightful country.

You burn no boats by becoming a permanent resident in Portugal. And there is no question, as some people seem to think, of renouncing your British citizenship. If you hold a British passport, you continue to use it, even though you are now domiciled in this country. If you want, for some reason, to stop living in Portugal, you simply hand your *Residência* back to the Immigration authorities.

With this probationary card, you are now entitled to many of the same considerations as a Portuguese resident of this country. It is no great hardship not being allowed to vote in local elections because they are almost impossible to understand. And in any case, if you register at the British Consulate before you have been out of the UK for five years, and providing you are a voter at home, you can now join in the British elections.

As a resident, you can now exchange your unprofitable Tourist Account for an interest-paying deposit account and a current one. You can get the ID card that allows you to set up in business. You can travel by train at reduced rates, if you are of pensionable age. (As a matter of fact, OAPs on holiday

The pleasant and peaceful fishing village of Ericeira had one historic moment in 1910, when the last king of Portugal fled from here to exile in England

Serra da Arrábida: the Convento Novo was founded by St Peter of Alcantara in the sixteenth century. (Below) The Madonna is carried through the streets in a festival procession

Óbidos was fortified by the Moors and by Dom Afonso
Henriques; the castle is now a state-run hotel

Nazaré is famous for its fishing village, native costumes and the
Chapel of Nossa Senhora de Nazaré, a centre of pilgrimage

(Above) The ancient frontier town of Monção in northern Portugal famous for its green wine and medicinal springs (Below) Coimbra was Portugal's capital city for 200 years, the Botanical Gardens are justly famous

The Vouga Valley landscape is one of densely wooded mountains and small riverside villages

(Opposite) A tiled house in Valença do Minho in the north of the country

A port wine boat at Oporto

Vila Real: the house on the Mateus wine label

here can also get reduced fares, but nobody seems to know that.)

However, you cannot yet buy more than half a hectare of land, as discussed in Chapter 4. And within six months of collecting your card you must not be caught driving a foreign-registered car, or with anything but a Portuguese driving licence.

You are now subject to Portugal's quite stringent currency controls, which change with alarming frequency. At the moment, no adult resident is allowed to take more than 50,000 escudos out of the country on any one trip. But they may take an additional 150,000 escudos' worth of foreign currency each time, and this 200,000 escudo total does not include any travel or hotel costs, nor do credit cards count.

When it comes to the time to renew your Type "A" *Residên-cia*, take it back to the *Serviço de Estrangeiros*, with 2,500 escudos to pay the fee and evidence that you can support yourself during the coming year. Your last three or four bank statements, showing a regular flow of pension or other money, for example, or a letter to that effect from your bank manager.

When you have held and renewed a Type "A" *Residência* for five years, you will be offered the Type "B" which costs 6,500 escudos and is renewable at five-year intervals. This is not only a good bargain in terms of time and hassle, but it also allows you to buy all the land you want or can afford.

There is also a Type "C" *Residência* which is issued after you have been officially resident in Portugal for twenty years and which, once you have it, lasts a lifetime without renewal. But information on the Type "C" is hard to come by because, as far as anyone can find out, such a thing has never been issued since *Residências* were first invented.

If for some reason you don't renew your card when you are supposed to, don't be surprised to find the police at your door. Or, if you are away, at your neighbour's door. If you have left the country for good, you should have surrendered your card. If you have merely forgotten or been away at the time, you will be asked to go and get your card renewed without delay, and be fined for being late.

Identity cards

With *Residência* in hand, you can now start getting your Portuguese identity card. Theoretically, you can deal with all the paperwork in one day, if you dash about a bit and if you are within easy reach of the Embassy or a Consulate. But that is theory and this is Portugal. In any event, you can certainly count on waiting at least a month after you have done your part and before receiving your card.

The very mention of identity cards is enough to send some people into orbit. They can have a very nasty connotation in totalitarian countries and in places like separatist Quebec, where the idea was suggested some years ago. In Portugal there is nothing sinister about the blue card with the unflattering photograph and the thumbprint. Everybody carries one of some colour, and it can be very useful.

For one thing, with a *Bilhete de Identidade* tucked in your wallet, you no longer have to lug your passport around or hand it over when registering at a Portuguese hotel. You can show your identity card with an application for a post office box (see Chapter 3) and the form will be countersigned without fuss. Even more to the point, you cannot get a Portuguese licence to drive without your identity card.

So it's back once again to the British Consulate, or to the Consular Section of the Embassy if you're living in the Lisbon area. Take passport, two (or in some areas, three) of those colour photographs and your *Residência*. Ask for a certificate with which to apply for an identity card.

The next step is to take all the papers to the President of the Parish Council (*Junta de Freguesia*) who will certify that you live where you say you live, namely in his parish. If you are lucky, this important gentleman may well have an office in or near the local town hall.

Ours lived a couple of villages away, and when we eventually found his house, he was out. Instinct and a small boy led us to the local pub, where he was discovered enjoying a beer. A most delightful gentleman, who was not at all put out to have his lunchtime ruined by customers. We sat for what seemed like hours in his tome-lined business room while he pecked laboriously at the oldest typewriter in captivity, transferring the same old information onto the official blue paper, chatting the while and exclaiming with interest at every other fact. The *Senhora* was born in Jerusalem? Imagine that! He knew someone who had a friend who had been to Jerusalem many years ago. It was indeed a small world. *Jornalistas?* He did not remember meeting any journalists before and was flatteringly chuffed to come across two in one day. When he discovered that by an odd coincidence he and my husband were exactly the same age, we had a full five-minute break for back-slapping, hand-shaking and congratulations all round before he went back to his hunt-and-peck typing.

Luckily we had lived in Portugal just long enough to have lost our North American habit of hurrying. What with this and that, by the time we had finished it was too late to take the completed papers to the *Conservatorio do Registo Civil* in the Town Hall. So we discussed the smallness of the world again, admired Senhor Fuzeta's garden and his fat tabby cat, shook hands some more and went home.

The next day we managed to complete our part of the exercise. A small, stern girl in the municipal notary's office received us and our papers with unsmiling efficiency. Then spoilt the whole effect by dissolving into giggles at the sight of our passport photographs. She filled in some more forms, relieved us of about 50 pence worth of escudos and said our *bilhetes* would be ready for collection in four weeks. (The price, by the way, has now gone up to 85 pence each.)

Perhaps they were. But we had got into the habit of allowing a few extra days for bureaucratic nonsenses and saving petrol and patience by avoiding fruitless journeys wherever possible. When we turned up five weeks later, our cards were ready to be signed and decorated with inky thumbprints.

When you have all three cards—*Cartão de Contribuinte*, *Residência* and *Bilhete de Identidade*—have them photo-copied and keep the copies in a safe place. If you should lose any or all of the originals, it will make replacement just a little easier if you can produce the photocopy.

A Portuguese driving licence
Once you receive your *Residência*, you have six months in

which to get a Portuguese driving licence. And one of those months is taken up waiting for your ID card to arrive.

Before this six-month grace period was introduced, just a short time ago, any number of foreigners were driving illegally and there was nothing they or anyone else could do about it. Even if they were driving Portuguese cars, they were technically law-breakers as they went home triumphantly with their new *Residências*. Because you had to have the two bits of paper at the same time, which everyone knew was impossible. You've never been able to apply for a driving licence without producing an ID card; and you can't produce that in less than a month.

However, with that ID card the business of exchanging your British licence for a Portuguese one is allegedly swifter and simpler than it used to be, and the whole thing can be accomplished in a week. But not by you, I would guess.

This is one instance when it really might be much better to go to a specialist. If there is a foreign residents' advisory service in your area, go and talk to them. They will charge you what looks like a huge amount of money to produce your Portuguese licence, but they can do it in a week, whereas it could easily take you months and cost just as much in time and travel.

Briefly—and there is actually nothing brief about this exercise—the procedure for getting a Portuguese licence to drive a car or a motor-bike over 50cc is as follows.

You take yourself, your *Residência*, *Bilhete de Identidade*, British driving licence, three passport photographs and any other piece of paper you can think of to the Consulate. There you get a certificate telling everyone that you can read and write to an acceptable Portuguese standard and that you have no criminal record. You then have to find the doctor in your own *Conselho* (Municipality) who does medical examinations for this special purpose, pass the test and have all the copies of the medical report notarized, and one copy deposited at the local Health Centre.

All the rest of the papers, plus photographs, then have to be taken to the *Secção de Viaço*, the Transport Department in the provincial capital, where there are more forms to be filled in, after which your British licence is taken away and you are given a provisional Portuguese one—a *Guia*.

What makes it even more tiresome is that both the Consular certificate and the doctor's report are valid only for a stated time. And not even the same stated time. So if you have not managed to get yourself medically examined before the Consular certificate expires, you have to go back to the Consulate for another one. Or if you are unable to get that handful of papers to the *Secção de Viaço* before either the certificate or the medical report expires, you have to start all over again. It's the Portuguese version of Snakes and Ladders, only worse.

People who specialize in this sort of thing have made it their business to gain quick access to the officials who do the signing. Turning up at the Department at precisely the right time and with a dozen licences to be processed, and with all the preliminary paperwork properly done, a professional licence-getter does not have to hang around for hours waiting his turn in the queue, as you or I would. Much better to pay a professional and concentrate on passing the medical examination, which is not too difficult. In that way you have a better-than-sporting chance of getting your Portuguese licence in a week and being able to drive with a clear conscience.

Eventually your permanent licence will arrive. But don't hold your breath. It may take as long as several months.

There is a drawback to driving with a Portuguese licence, permanent or provisional. You can only drive within Portugal. If you decide to drive back to Britain for a holiday, or even just over the border into Spain, you must first get an International Driving Licence from the Automóvel Clube de Portugal. Take your licence or *Guia*, one black-and-white passport photograph and 2,260 escudos to pay for it.

Don't forget that, if you are driving abroad, you need to have a Green Card from your insurance company. If you set off on a whim, however, you can always buy one at the border crossing.

You may very well be told by helpful acquaintances that it is perfectly legal to carry two driving licences here, one Portuguese and one British—thereby avoiding all the bother of getting an International one if you are leaving the country. It is not. And if the police see you carrying a British licence as well as a Portuguese one, they are not going to be amused, because your British licence was officially handed in to the authorities. However, as every British driver well knows, should a licence be lost, the owner only has to write to the Drivers and Vehicles Licensing Centre, Swansea SA99 1AB, giving the licence particulars and they will very obligingly send a replacement.

When you get here, it might be a good idea to make contact with the nearest office of the ACP, either in Lisbon or at one of their branches in Faro, Oporto, Coimbra and Aveiro. They will be able to tell you if there have been any changes in licence-getting or any other motoring matter.

Licences for bikes, etc.
You will be glad to know that you do not have to trek all the way to the provincial capital to get a licence for either a moped (under 50cc) or a bicycle. Both of these can be obtained from the local *Câmara*.

If you bring bicycles from Britain, get them licensed before you go riding around on them. To complete the green registration card, you need to know the make of the machine, the size (1.17m seems to be the standard bike size here), the year it was made, what kind of frame it has (normal, very likely); the size of the front and rear wheels (probably 26 × 13/8—which looks odd, but that's what my bike licence says), the weight of the machine itself and how much weight it can carry. Also its colour. Take these facts to the *Câmara* and for a very small sum you will be issued with the *livrete* (registration card) and a yellow-and-black plate which is attached to the back of the bicycle.

If it is a motorized model, the *Câmara* will want to know all about the engine: the brand, number, cylinders, etc. And you will be shown some standard road signs to identify before you get your *livrete*.

At the back of the registration booklet there are some reminders. Carry the card with you when you are riding the machine. If you make alterations to it, the vehicle has to be inspected and the *livrete* altered to match. If you move house, move out of the Municipality, sell the machine or decide that your bicycling days are over, the *Câmara* should be told within thirty days.

It will come as no surprise to learn that you can't just sell your bike casually, as you would at home. It has to be done officially, with official paper, fiscal stamps, changes of registration and all the rest of it.

Dogs are supposed to be licensed, though very few Portuguese ones are. When yours has its first annual rabies injection (see Chapter 11), you take the vet's certificate to the *Câmara* and apply. A properly legalized dog wears a large metal tag on its collar, for which you pay 800 escudos; guard and hunting dogs are licensed for half that price.

Paper-chasing does take time if you do it all yourself. But at least you learn your way around the *Câmara*, which is always useful; and you gradually get to know the city officials, which can be even more useful. We enjoyed our paper-go-round and felt quite triumphant when we had gathered all our documents.

Registration of visitors

However, we were not quite as legal as we thought. After four Portuguese summers, during which the flat was full of friends and family (it's amazing how popular you suddenly become when you live in a foreign holiday resort), we discovered we had been breaking the law with great regularity.

When you have visitors, even family visitors, they must be registered with the police, in exactly the same way as all European hotels register their guests.

Again, there is nothing sinister or Big Brother about this. It is simply a safeguard. If a visitor to Portugal should be taken suddenly ill or become involved in an accident, the police naturally need to know where that visitor is staying. Registration is also a way of keeping tabs on the annual tourism figures—essential statistics in a country that relies so heavily on holidaymakers for its national bread and butter.

As soon as you hear guests are in the offing, go to the *Serviço de Estrangeiros* and buy a bunch of registration cards: *Boletims Individual de Alojomento*. They cost about 10 escudos each, and you can buy as many as you think you will need to get you through the holiday season.

Ask your visitors to complete the front of the card, including the rather repetitive stub. And do this as soon as you decently can after they arrive; cards ought to be handed in to the police within forty-eight hours of your guests' arrival. They are not difficult to complete. The first line wants to know nationality and surname (*apelido*), the second their Christian names. On the third line put the town of birth (*nascido a*) and the date (*em*). Then come the passport particulars. Tick the box marked *passaporte* and fill in the number (*No.*) *Valido até* means "valid until" and requires a date. Where you see *emitado em*, write the town where the passport was issued. The last section wants to know the date of entry into Portugal (*data entrada em Portugal*) and where (*posto de fronteira*) which will usually be the name of an airport or frontier crossing. Visitors should sign where it says *assinatura*. The perforated tab needs a date filled in, the name and nationality of the visitor (twice) and the date of their departure.

You fill in the back of the card with the date, the town or village where you live and finally your name and full address. Take these cards to the nearest police station, where an officer will stamp everything and hand you back one of the perforated bits.

By the end of the summer you will probably have quite a collection of these small bits of card. Keep them somewhere safe and relatively handy, where they can be found without too much fuss if an official suddenly turns up and asks to see them. It is most unlikely that this will ever happen, but all kinds of officials are empowered to make spot checks—including tax officials, who can drop in on people who work at home to see that their books are properly kept.

So far, touch wood, it has not happened to us, but we keep every bit of Portuguese paper that is even slightly official, just to be on the safe side. And to prove that we are doing our best, however inefficiently.

10. Earning a Living

Not all foreigners come to Portugal to live on their pensions. A recent report said that the emigration patterns are changing, especially in the Algarve, which is now attracting an increasing number of young people who are moving here to earn a living in the sun. And many of those who did originally come to retire from the rat-race and who planned on doing nothing more energetic than a little golf or gentle gardening often change their minds. After a spell of vegetation many start looking around for something to do, either to keep busy or to bring in a few extra escudos.

But the fact that you have been granted a Residence Visa does not automatically entitle you to take a job in Portugal. To do that you must have a proper work permit and, though it is very slightly easier to acquire one of those in 1987 than it was in 1984—now that more foreign companies are investing in Portugal, since its entry into the EEC—it is still not easy.

Portugal, of course, has only just started on the ten-year transition period which leads up to fully-integrated membership of the European Economic Community and, in 1987, there are still quite severe restrictions on foreigners coming here to work. These will eventually disappear and it looks as though deregulation will begin in 1990 because, by the end of that year, the transition calendar calls for an examination of the success of this trial period of free circulation of workers within the member countries.

In the mean time, and like so many other western countries, Portugal has a painfully high rate of unemployment. There are simply not enough jobs to go round and, to make matters worse, many young people are now leaving the family farms to look for work in the cities. This is particularly true in the Algarve, with its coastline of holiday towns and tourist developments. In the summer, you very seldom see any young men at work in the fields. They and their sisters are either looking for work or have managed to find jobs among the bright lights of the coastal resorts, where the pay can be better than average and there is a certain amount of what passes for glamour. Sadly, a high proportion of these more glamorous jobs come to an abrupt halt at the end of the tourist season.

In this situation, the authorities are obviously going to do their best to see that any available jobs go to qualified Portuguese nationals, which is only right. But it does mean that you cannot rely on getting a permit to hold a job here as, for example, a receptionist, salesman or bookkeeper—even if you speak fluent Portuguese. If you have been working in Britain as a waiter or a dental assistant, a taxi-driver or a typesetter, you may have trouble getting a permit to continue your line of work when you get to Portugal, because there are qualified Portuguese who can fill any of these jobs.

There are foreigners who are employed in Portugal, of course, but they usually have some extra qualifications that a Portuguese national may not have, or they are employed by a foreign-owned company, though a foreign organization in Portugal is not allowed to staff itself entirely with its own compatriots. The official ratio is ten to one—ten Portuguese employees for every foreigner.

Work permits

A Portuguese work permit is not just a stamp in a foreign passport. It is a contract, approved by the Portuguese Ministry of Labour, between the employer and employee, and it lasts for six months. After that time it can usually be renewed with no trouble. But if the employee leaves that company before the six months are up, and takes a job elsewhere, a new contract has to be made with the new employer.

It is the employer's responsibility to see that a work permit is applied for and granted. If you are offered a job once you have settled here, make very sure that the permit is in order, and don't necessarily believe it if you are told that no permit is required for whatever it is you are going to do. The fines for working here illegally are quite heavy.

With the high unemployment figures in Portugal, you may wonder, as we did, about the many young foreigners you see working in bars and restaurants in the tourist areas during the season. How did these people obtain work permits for jobs that could quite well be done by young Portuguese? Some of them obviously did not. But it is possible to get permission, as a tourist, to have a working holiday—providing the temporary employer informs the Ministry of Labour.

Professional people—doctors, dentists, lawyers and so on—are not allowed to move to Portugal, hang out their shingle and go to work on the strength of their British qualifications. Not even if they speak Portuguese. They must present their credentials to the appropriate Portuguese body, who may or may not grant permission to practise.

Self-employment

As a foreigner, it is difficult to obtain employment in Portugal, but there is nothing to stop your going into business for yourself and, as long as you have your papers proclaiming you a permanent resident, you need no work permit to do this. All you need is a small stamp in your passport from the *Serviço de Estangeiros*, for which you pay 500 escudos.

The Algarve is a wonderful area for entrepreneurs and innovators because, compared to Lisbon and Oporto, it is still fairly unsophisticated. Also because it is almost entirely geared to the tourist industry, and tourists need goods and services.

There are dozens of British, Dutch, German, Scandinavian and American residents along the Algarve coast, all in business for themselves and doing very nicely, most of them. They run bars, restaurants, discos, boutiques, delicatessens, garden centres, advisory services, clubs, pubs, guesthouses, newspapers and riding stables. They breed poultry and cage birds, they market-garden, service cars, board animals, manage holiday villas, organize boat trips, teach languages, sell property, develop land, build and run sports centres. There are foreigners, too, who work hard at more solitary occupations: the artists, photographers, potters, writers, sculptors and those who make jewellery, carve wood and weave for fun and profit.

The American who introduced the Algarve's first laundrette was onto a good thing, and he has been coining it in ever since. Well, ever since he finally managed to get the operation licensed and properly equipped with the machines and an adequate supply of gas, water and electricity. All of which took a ridiculously long time, to his American way of thinking.

In those days, the concept of self-service was something quite new to the Algarve. Come to that, there was not much service of any kind until the *retornados* from the African colonies began to move to this province, bringing with them up-to-date ideas from large modern cities like Luanda and Lourenço Marques.

When a couple of businessmen from Mozambique set up an agricultural and veterinary supplies shop, they also introduced after-sales service for their customers. The local farmers were surprised and delighted to think that anyone cared enough about the welfare of their pigs and the state of their crops to call in on them from time to time, and they became very faithful customers. The Mozambiquans attracted a number of non-farming customers to their shop too, by installing the district's first commercial photocopying machine. All the local offices used it, and you would see businessmen browsing through the shelves of farming supplies, maybe buying some seed or a curry-comb, while they awaited their turn at the copier. Now every town has at least half a dozen places where you can pop in and get photocopies made for 10 escudos a page.

If your time-filling or income-producing idea has to do with tourism, be prepared to work frantically during the summer, when it can be exceedingly hot and every coastal town is stiff with visitors. Those who run bars and restaurants here, or who take tourists on game-fishing and sightseeing trips, reckon they have from May to October to make their year's money. After October, visitors come to the Algarve in dribbles rather than hordes and, apart from a short-lived burst of activity around Christmas and Easter, the province is quiet in winter.

The golfers come to Portugal in winter, and the Algarve courses are busy. But until it is more widely known that this southern province is a perfect place to spend the off-season, and until there is more to occupy the non-golfing winter visitors, the year's hard work in the tourist trade is done in the summer.

Licences

Unless you are going to be working quietly at home—painting, writing, weaving or whatnot—you would be wise to assume that you are going to need some sort of licence to earn a living. You may not, but it is a great deal better to spend a little time checking this than to be found operating illegally, however innocently.

In this last year, the Portuguese authorities have become much more strict about unlicensed activities of all kinds, and about documentation in general. Check with someone in a position to know about such things—the Consul, your bank manager, lawyer, a tax official, the *Serviço de Estrangeiros* —about the necessity for a licence for your particular activity. Better still, ask them all, and if three of them give you the same answer, you can be reasonably sure it is the right one.

You will certainly need a licence to embark on any form of activity that has to do with the sea: fishing trips, water sports, sightseeing excursions. And your first approach may have to be made to the *Cabo do Mar*, the uniformed Beach Master. But the man who has the last word on any maritime project, after you have ploughed through all the paperwork and red tape, is the *Capitão do Porto*, the Harbour Master, who is usually responsible for an enormous stretch of coastline and everything that goes on along it, from multi-million-escudo harbour improvements to the rental of paddleboats.

The *Capitão do Porto* may have his own reasons for refusing a licence. When two young Germans applied to ours some years ago for a licence to open a diving school, he turned them down. Not because they were under-qualified or because he disapproved of their boat or diving equipment but because he knew that this particular corner of the Algarve did not have the facilities to cope with any diving accidents at that time.

If you are thinking of bringing your boat to Portugal and making a living with it, check first about the procedure for changing it to a Portuguese registration before you even think about licences.

You don't need a licence to open a shop, unless you are selling food. Then you do. And anyone who handles food, in a shop or restaurant, must be checked for tuberculosis annually.

If you want to open a restaurant, a new one, application must first be made to the Ministry of Tourism in Lisbon. If they agree that the area could stand another restaurant, approval then has to be given by the Civil Governor of the province, the local *Câmara* and the local health authorities. There are pages of regulations and rules that must be observed before a final licence is granted: the bar must be well separated from the dining area, the loos equipped with paper towels and liquid soap dispensers—the list goes on for ever. If you have visited some of the less pretentious Portuguese eating places, this may come as a surprise. I can think of half a dozen that would be closed on the spot if an inspector showed up. But once again, what the Portuguese do about bending the rules in their own country is their business. As foreigners, we have to lean over backwards to observe those rules.

One rule is currently being broken on a massive scale, and for the most part by foreigners. In the Algarve there is a great deal of ill-feeling in high places about people who are merrily renting out holiday accommodation without first registering the fact. It is claimed that there are more "black" tourist beds than legal ones, which of course means a substantial loss of tax income for Portugal. If you are planning to rent your villa or take in boarders, find out first about licences.

Buying a business
If you are looking around for a business to buy, buy one that is already licensed and operating.

That is the advice of an Englishman who used to run the most popular disco around here. He thought he was cutting through the worst of the red tape when, with a Portuguese partner, he bought a building that had already been approved for conversion into a disco. But the battle was far from won. Even with a Portuguese lawyer and a Portuguese accountant at his elbow—both of which, he says, are absolutely essential in any sort of business enterprise—it was two full years before he got his licence to operate legally. In spite of all the early frustrations, the disco did extremely well, because the owner really knew his trade, having built and operated four similar establishments in Britain before he ever thought of coming to Portugal. When he sold out to someone who had never been in the disco business, the whole thing went down the drain.

Sticking to what you know

If you can devise a way to use your professional talents in Portugal, you should be able to make a living. Not a large living by British standards, but then you don't need so much money to live comfortably here. It is the people who stray away from their own trade who usually come to grief.

Unless you have professional experience, forget any pie-in-the-sky ideas about coming to Portugal—and, more particularly, to the Algarve—and opening a bar. For one thing, there are already plenty of bars and you may not get a licence. For another, you will find out the hard way that running a bar in a foreign country is much more difficult than it looks.

Similarly, the fact that you have spent more years than you care to remember preparing delicious meals in your own kitchen does not necessarily qualify you to cook profession-ally. "An intimate little restaurant" is another widespread pipedream, and quite a few local restaurateurs have told us with varying degrees of vehemence that the next soon-to-retire businessman, bookie or boilermaker who thinks that he and his wife could run one will get, at best, an earful.

If you are casting around for something profitable to do in Portugal, take your time about it. Study the area carefully. See what it already has in the way of businesses and amenities, and what is missing. Maybe you are qualified and capable of filling one of the gaps.

And don't think only in terms of the tourist trade, even in the holiday areas. Remember the residents, both Portuguese and foreign, and consider whether you could provide something that they need. A steady, year-round business would be less exhausting than one that depended primarily on a frenetic summer season.

One good piece of advice comes from an Algarve resident who has settled here after half a lifetime of doing business all over the world. Use the Portuguese resources, he says, and don't get embroiled in importing or exporting. In the present economic situation, the duty on all imported goods is crippling and the paperwork incredible. On top of that, delivery can be difficult, and you can find the consignment you need so urgently is held up in Customs.

Some people have been able to take their hobbies and turn them into money-making concerns. An enthusiastic gardener here has just received an order to design and plant dozens of windowboxes for a villa development. Last time we saw her, she was knee-deep in geraniums and petunias, mixing and matching like mad.

Telling the tax-man

To repeat: you do not need a work permit if you are self-employed, as a one-man show. But as soon as you are set to make money, you must register the fact at the local tax office.

Take your *Residência*, *Cartão de Contribuinte* and *Bilhete de Identidade* and explain (or, if possible, show) what you are going to do. There will be a form to complete, of course, and your enterprise will be categorized and you will be entered on the tax roll.

Freelance workers—painters, writers, photographers and people who make and sell things—must be careful to keep accurate records of payment. For this you will probably need a book of official receipts (*Carderneta de Recibos*) obtainable for a small sum from the local tax office, and a *Registo de Receitas e Despesas*, an A4-sized ruled ledger that can be bought from a stationery shop. Your accountant will show you how to fill them both in, and warn you against making a mess of the numbered receipts.

Now that Portugal belongs to the EEC, we are blessed with the Portuguese version of VAT. IVA means exactly the same thing, works in the same way and is just as much of a headache.

However, the introduction of IVA was not all bad for those people who made and sold things, or who supplied any sort of a service. It did away with two other headaches which had bedevilled small business people: the *Imposto de Selo* or stamp tax, which involved much licking and sticking and working out of 0.3 per cent on receipts, and the 17 per cent transaction tax that applied to just about anything that was imported or made.

The standard rate of IVA is 16 per cent in mainland Portugal (Madeira and the Azores get away with 12 per cent) and there is a reduced rate of 8 per cent on some goods and services including processed food, fuel, communications and rentals. Luxury items are charged IVA at 30 per cent, but there is no tax on unprocessed food, medicines, books and some professional services.

If you're going into business in Portugal and even if you are well acquainted with VAT, it would be unwise to do your own IVA. For one thing, you'll never manage the Portuguese forms and, for another, it is supposed to be done by an accountant.

If you go into partnership and run a home-based business —one that does not require a shop or an office, merely some working space and (with luck) a telephone—it is advisable to be registered with the Ministry of Justice in Lisbon as "Collective People", or words to that effect. Your enterprise is entered on the tax files and given a number which you use for billing and tax purposes, and the partnership is issued with a card —just one card—that is renewable every four years. Your lawyer or accountant will help you with the inevitable form which is sent off to the capital with all the particulars about who you are, what you do and where you do it. After a decent interval, the *Cartão de Identificação de Entidade Equiparada a Pessoa Colectiva* will arrive through the mail.

Though you will now pay *Contribuição Industrial*, the tax that is levied on all industrial or commercial activities, you do better in the way of allowable business expenses as Collective People than you do as a solo operator. Find an accountant who speaks enough English to help you through all this, and who will keep your books and file your tax returns. There are so many little rules about monetary matters that it is very much better to pay someone who knows how to do everything correctly.

For anything more advanced than Collective People—if you

want to form a company, for example, or negotiate for business premises—you certainly need a lawyer, just as you would in Britain.

With legal and accounting help, a bit of imagination and a large helping of patience, there is nothing to prevent your earning a living in Portugal. Be prepared, however, to work harder than you ever did at home and for everything to take much, much longer than you expect.

11. Taking Care

It is extraordinary what an effect the sun seems to have on some people.

In the same way that otherwise sane and businesslike foreigners will cheerfully buy property without the help of a solicitor, any number of expatriates will spend a great deal of money buying or building a house in the sun—and never get around to insuring it. Perhaps it has something to do with Portugal's reputation as a relatively crime-free country, compared with other European ones. It is true that reported incidents of robbery and crimes of violence are nothing like as frequent as they are in Britain, but even so, it is madness to tempt providence.

And speaking of providence, what about those Acts of God? When the big rains came to the Lisbon-Estoril-Cascais area in winter of 1983, devastating the towns and countryside, the majority of the people who lost their homes were not covered by insurance.

There are plenty of Portuguese companies who will write policies on your house, car and other possessions. Império and Aliança are two of the largest, with branches all over the country. Look in the Yellow Pages under *Seguros-Companhias*. If you think you would feel more comfortable with a familiar English name, look also in the English-language press for people like Eagle Star, Prudential and Royal Exchange. Many of their agents in Portugal are either expatriates or English-speaking Portuguese.

A Portuguese policy is a little different from the one you are used to in Britain. For one thing, it needs to be revised more often, because, although there is certainly inflation in this country, there are no automatic inflation-linked increases in insurance policies. There has been talk of it, but so far nothing has happened.

Your house and its contents can be covered, but not the land it stands on. Included in the building are such things as gates, garage, pool and solar-heating fixtures. By "contents", a Portuguese insurance company means anything that can be moved.

The house is valued for insurance purposes at the amount it would cost to rebuild. In the Algarve, this is sómething in the region of 40,000 escudos a square metre, depending on who does the rebuilding and where the house is situated. You may well find the cost is lower in northern Portugal. If you have to have all or part of your house rebuilt, the insurance company will normally pay for alternative accommodation until the house is habitable again. But they will set a limit on both the length of time and the cost of your stay in a hotel.

When it comes to the contents, you insure them for the cost of replacement in Portugal. Most companies here put a limit on the amount they will pay out for any one item—five per cent of the total value of the contents. So if your belongings are insured for a flat one million escudos and your 100,000 escudo video is pinched, you will not get more than 50,000 escudos in compensation.

It is not wise to under-insure your possessions, or to let your policy become out of date. If you collect expensive things such as furniture, paintings, jewellery, etc., make sure they are immediately included in the policy, even though that will mean an increase in premiums. If you should have to make a claim and the company feels you are under-insured, they are entitled to reduce their payment on your claim.

You can cover your house and its contents against most of the usual disasters: fire, flood, earthquakes, gas explosions and burglary—which means that the house has been broken into before anything is stolen, so an open door or window could nullify the claim.

Some insurance companies have their own ideas about damage. Friends in the village had what could have been a very nasty accident with a portable gas heater with a perished pipe, which burst into flames one evening. As it happened and thanks entirely to swift action on the part of a neighbour, who heaved the flaming contraption down a flight of stairs and into the road, the only thing that was seriously damaged was the heater itself. But the insurance company would only pay for "damage caused" and that did not apparently include the heater. All they would pay out for was one slightly singed rug.

Check your policy and make very sure what the company will and will not pay out for. Check too that the supply pipe on any gas-driven gadget is always in good repair, especially if it comes, as that one did, as part of the furniture and fittings in a newly acquired home.

You can insure against the unlikely event that an aeroplane will fall on your house. And against the much more likely event that a car will crash into it. But it has to be someone else's car, and you cannot claim against insurance if you hit your own house while backing out of the garage.

You can claim if a sudden rainstorm damages the roof or ceilings. But if the assessor finds that the damage is not as sudden as the rainstorm, that it has accumulated over a period of time, you will probably have an argument on your hands. You are expected to keep your property in good repair.

One of our leading Algarve insurance men advises every property-owner to have good locks on doors and windows. Breaking and entering is not as prevalent in Portugal as in other countries, but the statistics for crime creep up slowly every year, sadly.

If you are nervous or have a house full of expensive belongings, you might want to look into the question of alarm systems. A glance through the papers will point you towards the companies that instal these devices and, if you live in a well-policed area, an alarm may be a good idea. In some parts of Portugal, though, the police response is not yet as swift as it might be. A couple of large, ferocious-looking guard dogs might be just as effective.

If you plan to rent your Portuguese home during the holiday season, you should take out special insurance. You are not responsible for the holiday tenants' possessions, but it is advisable to provide cover for accidents and injury resulting from some defect in the building. A falling tile, for example.

Car insurance

When we arrived in Portugal, we were dismayed to learn that drivers were not then obliged to carry third-party insurance. So most people didn't. Luckily the law was changed soon afterwards, and now, if you are stopped in a routine road-check, one of the papers the police want to see is the receipt for your current year's insurance.

Again, be careful not to under-insure your car, because, if it becomes involved in an accident, your claim will be under-paid in exactly the same proportion. For example, a million-escudo Triumph Acclaim covered for three-quarters of its value may suffer, say, half a million escudos' worth of damage. But the company will pay out only three-quarters of that half million escudos—375,000 escudos.

Your Portuguese policy gives you a flat-rate reduction on your premium after two claim-free years.

If you are ever involved in a road accident, you will have to keep your cool if you are to stand a chance of getting full recompense from your insurance company. In some cases, but by no means all, the Latin temperament comes frothing to the fore, and everyone, including the crowd that materializes out of nowhere, becomes intensely dramatic.

The police must be called at once if anyone is hurt. Or if the other driver refuses to give you his particulars. Or if he does not have a valid insurance certificate. If there is any sort of an argument about responsibility, call the cops immediately. Whatever you do, do not be bullied or cajoled into moving either of the vehicles before the police have arrived. While you are waiting for them to turn up and draw chalk marks all over the road, take your own notes about the accident so that you can give your insurance company all the details. Note the position of both vehicles in regard to the curb and the white line on the road. Pace the skid marks, the distance from any traffic signs and parked vehicles.

Both drivers are obliged by law to exchange details of insurance companies and policy numbers. Take a good look at the other driver's policy to see that it is up to date. Unless the accident was unarguably your fault, don't admit liability. Instead, try to find a reliable witness among the excited onlookers, someone prepared to make a statement about the accident. Reliable witnesses to anything are as thin on the ground in Portugal as they are anywhere else, but you may be able to get a name and an address. Claim within eight days of any accident.

If you have full coverage and are accepting liability, claiming for your own damages, you put your car in a garage, and an assessor will turn up to agree an estimate for repairs. You will have to pay a *franquia*, an initial charge on any claim, which may be one or two per cent of the repairs cost, depending on the age of your car.

If you have full coverage but do not accept responsibility, your insurance company will try to recover the cost of your damages from the other driver's insurers. If they cannot reach an agreement, the case goes to arbitration by the *Câmara de Arbitragem* and a decision will eventually be reached.

"Eventually" is the operative word in any matter before the Portuguese courts, and one Portuguese gentleman recently became so enraged at the six-year delay in settling his arbitration case that he appealed to the European Commission of Human Rights at Strasbourg. The Commission agreed that he was indeed being deprived of his rights, since no insurance payment could be made to him until after the court verdict. They have now referred the matter to the European Court, to decide how much compensation he should receive.

If you carry only third-party insurance, you are on your own when it comes to claiming for damages. You have to deal with the other driver's company and, if they are unhelpful, you will need a lawyer if you are going to pursue the matter.

As yet, there is no "knock-for-knock" agreement among Portuguese insurance companies, as there is in most other European countries. British companies in Portugal, though, will apparently pay up without a quibble to clients holding their fully comprehensive policies.

Insure yourself to the eyebrows and drive very, very carefully.

Medical insurance
This is something you will probably have arranged before you

left Britain (see Chapter 6). For anyone already holding private insurance in the UK, this is merely a matter of getting re-classified as an expatriate member of BUPA, PPP or similar organization.

Some people don't bother about medical insurance when they come to Portugal, assuming that the British Consular people will come to their rescue if they become suddenly ill. They won't. Much as they might like to, British Consular officials are not allowed to help out with medical or hospital bills for expatriates. The best they can do in a case of really dire emergency is to arrange for a British resident in Portugal to be sent back for treatment in Britain—always providing he is not too ill to travel. And always on the understanding that repayment is made immediately, if not sooner.

The Embassy or Consulate will also want to be quite sure that there is nobody back in Britain—relatives, friends, even ex-employers—who can be called upon to make the travel arrangements and pay the fare. And that fare can be enormous, because it may be necessary to pay for four or five aircraft seats, if they are removed to make room for a stretcher. On top of which, there is the air fare for the doctor, nurse or attendant who accompanies the patient. Which is bad enough, but it can get even worse. If it is not possible to fly a patient back to Britain by scheduled airline, the only alternative is to charter a Jet Air Ambulance at a frightening cost.

It is much cheaper to be well covered for all manner of medical emergencies, so that you can receive treatment in Portugal without having to worry about paying the bill. You can also take out a policy to cover repatriation back to Britain for medical attention, but the premiums are quite steep.

There are several companies that will sell you peace of mind at reasonable rates. One of them, Exeter Hospital Aid Society (5 & 7 Princes Gate, Exeter EX1 1UE), will look after all charges for hospital care, surgery, convalescence and nursing at home for a single person, married couple or family. They will refund you for consultations and X-rays and for half the cost of any medicines prescribed. The cost of premiums varies according to the coverage you want and your age. There are other companies, too. If you have not organized any medical insurance by the time you get to Portugal, the British Hospital in Lisbon will give you a list of private insurers. Write to them at Rua Saraiva de Carvalho 49, Lisboa.

Though you may have jogged along nicely without any private insurance in Britain, remember that you will have to pay the fare from Portugal if you want to take advantage of the NHS after you move here. Remember, too, that it is a great deal more difficult to get a flight from Portugal on short notice, especially if you are living in the south.

If you are legally employed in Portugal, with a work permit to prove it, the company will make monthly deductions from your salary for payment to the *Caixa de Previdência*. This will entitle you to the same health insurance benefits as a Portuguese employee: free or substantially reduced medical attention and a discount on any prescribed medicines.

Self-employed people should also pay into *Caixa*, at a rate of twenty-nine per cent of the current minimum wage. Then they too are entitled to *Caixa* benefits. If you are retired or otherwise eligible for UK social security, register with the *Serviço Medico Sociais* and the local health centre (*Centro de Saúde*) and you can take advantage of the Portuguese health scheme.

If you employ anyone domestically—maids, cooks, gardeners—you will have to pay their *Caixa* (see Chapter 12) and you are legally responsible for any loss they may incur as a result of an accident at work. You might want to discuss this point with your insurance company.

Still on the subject of insurance, do encourage anyone who comes to stay with you to arrange for their own insurance when they are making their travel arrangements. Or, if you are reluctant to do this, make sure that holidaying guests are covered by your own policy. If someone breaks a leg or is suddenly rushed off to have an appendix removed, you could be lumbered with the bill.

Staying healthy
Even in this kindly climate, illness and accidents can happen and, without getting too hypochondriacal about it, it is as well to be prepared.

You might find, as we did, that the change in climate and

way of life makes you fair game for a whole new set of germs and viruses. Our first winter here was one continuous virulent cold, and one or both of us snuffled and sneezed from Christmas to Easter. Our second winter was slightly better, and we managed to avoid one or two of the bugs that were doing the rounds. By the third winter, our antibodies appeared to have pulled themselves together, and we were back to our normal healthy selves.

Bring with you a good supply of whatever you favour to deal with coughs, colds, sore throats, assorted aches and pains and seasonal queasies. Once you know your way around the area, you will find everything you need to cope with minor problems in a *farmácia*.

Many of the Portuguese chemists speak English, and they are extremely helpful. When you run out of an English remedy for whatever ails you, if you take the container to the *farmácia*, the chemist will almost certainly be able to produce something with all the essential ingredients, and he may even carry the same product. We were pleased to find we could buy Bayolin here, to deal with rheumaticky pains—at half the British price.

What you can and cannot buy over the counter depends on the *farmácia* you patronize. Some will not part with a packet of Vitamin C tablets without written authority and obviously hate to sell anything more medical than suntan lotion. But a town of any size usually has more than one chemist, so case these as carefully as you check everything else.

Among the pharmaceuticals you may find hard to get here are paracetamol and distalgesics. One item you do not need to bring is Alka-Seltzer or anything else to get yourself together after a night on the town. Fizzy, lemon-flavoured Guronsan tablets, made in Portugal, are the most effective cure we have ever found both for hangovers and for those miserable pre-cold blahs.

Several people have asked us recently if it is possible to get salt-free salt, the stuff you use if you have high blood-pressure. It is, and it is called Xal, but it is sometimes in short supply.

If you are suddenly taken ill or have an accident that cannot be dealt with out of the medicine cupboard, go straight to the Emergency Department (*Urgências*) of your local hospital.

Take your passport, or *Residência* and/or *Bilhete de Identidade*, and a dictionary or Portuguese-speaking friend in case there is a language difficulty. You can also get emergency treatment at a *Centro de Enfermagem* (Nursing Station) or a *Cruz Vermelha Portuguesa* (Red Cross Post) if there is one in your town. The staff at both these organizations will give injections, too.

If you have no transport, call an ambulance by dialling 115 on the nearest phone. This is the countrywide number for all emergencies, the equivalent to Britain's 999.

Of course you may have been clever enough to find a family doctor who makes house calls. Many of them do, even in the Algarve. In Canada, only the vets made house calls.

Living in the Lisbon or Oporto area, you will be well served by hospitals, clinics and medical specialists of all kinds. In the Algarve, there are major hospitals in Lagos, Portimão and Faro, with a number of much smaller ones in other towns.

But the number of doctors in the Algarve seems to be increasing every year, and quite a few of them, like the orthopaedic surgeon we met recently, have trained or worked in British hospitals and speak flawless English. Which is comforting. When you need a doctor, you do not need to be floundering around in a foreign language. Specialized clinics are also appearing in the once-backward Algarve. Only two years ago, local kidney patients had to travel to Lisbon for their dialysis treatment. Now there is a fine new centre in Faro and another smaller one in Portimão—which also has the most efficient radiography clinic I have ever seen.

As soon as you get to Portugal, or even before, start collecting names and information about doctors, specialists and your local hospital facilities. If you have all this at your fingertips, you are less likely to need any of them.

Many expatriates living in the Algarve subscribe to the British Hospital in Lisbon (see page 233), a small cottage-type hospital which has been in existence for more than 250 years and which was originally founded for the benefit of British merchant seamen. For a very modest subscription, members receive excellent treatment at extremely low charges in this fine little hospital where all the staff speak English.

Four winters ago, when an eighty-year-old American visitor fell and broke her hip, her daughter immediately summoned an ambulance to take the poor lady from Lagos to Lisbon, a journey of some 275 kilometres. She was operated on most successfully at the British Hospital, and the surgeon's bill was 40,000 escudos, which, at the time, was a little less than £250. The cost of the ambulance journey was 7,000 escudos, then about £40.

The British Hospital also has out-patient clinics six days a week. To become a member, all you have to do is fill in their enrolment form.

Eyes and teeth

Dentists, outside Lisbon and Oporto, may be slightly more difficult. Apparently Portugal is sadly under-dentisted, and it was even suggested recently that some are practising here without a proper licence.

Fortunately for us, there is an excellent Englishman in business in this neighbourhood. So when my husband broke a tooth we naturally phoned his office for an appointment. He was away for a month. And because we had not thought to investigate more than the one dentist, we had to waste time consulting friends before we could find someone to deal with the very painful emergency. When three different people recommended the same Portuguese dentist, we set off to find his surgery—decorated, to our dismay, with the most horrific posters about the dreadful things that can happen to teeth and gums. I lost my nerve completely, turned tail and fled to wait in a nearby coffee shop until it was all over.

In Portugal, it seems, you cannot judge a dentist by his taste in artwork. Michael emerged beaming and said that after a bit of a wait in a room full of Portuguese ladies exchanging gory details, he had received first-class treatment at a quarter of the price that our Canadian dentist would have charged.

Serious eye problems might be best dealt with in Lisbon, but if it is simply a matter of getting new glasses, there is bound to be at least one optician in the nearest town.

In ours, Senhor Silva does straightforward tests for reading and distance glasses, in the middle of the small shop where he also sells cameras and films. By the time he has slipped the first lens into the metal holder and handed you something incomprehensibly Portuguese to read, a small crowd has gathered to enjoy the show and give unwarranted advice about your choice of frames. If the necessary lenses are in stock and you don't insist on anything too fancy in the way of frames, you will be able to collect your new glasses within the hour, and at a cost that is more than reasonable.

For a more intensive test, Senhor Silva takes you round the corner to his apartment, where he has all the gadgets needed to check more complicated problems. If necessary, he will refer you to a specialist.

When we came here, Senhor Silva was the only optician in town. Now there are two other establishments, in flossier surroundings, where you can have your eyes checked in comparative privacy and without having to pause while someone buys a roll of film. I don't know if the rival firms are any more efficient, or if they can produce new glasses quicker than Senhor Silva, but they can't be nearly so entertaining.

Veterinary services
One of the reasons we chose to live in Portugal, as against any of the southern European countries or the West Indies, was that it seemed as though Portuguese people took care of their animals. There were—and still are, of course—stray dogs and cats, but they seem to find food and are nothing to compare with the walking toastracks that haunt the Caribbean beaches.

Long before we made the final decision to move to the Algarve, we made enquiries among the local animal-lovers and were assured that veterinary care was the least of our worries. One of the best small-animal vets in Europe, they told us, practised in the Algarve, within easy driving distance of the village. He still does, thank heavens, and he has since been joined by several other well-qualified vets, Portuguese practitioners who have come from the African colonies. Some are excellent, some are not. So, if you are planning to bring your pets, look around for the best man or woman practising in your area, because animals, unlike humans, cannot be repatriated for medical treatment in Britain.

Not all the vets in private practice are licensed to give the annual rabies injections that are required by law. Every spring the municipal vets tour the towns and villages, and every dog over six months old is rounded up, attached to a bit of string and brought along to be jabbed. Watch out for a printed notice stuck up in some prominent place in your community. It will have a thick red diagonal line across it and the headline *"Raiva"* (Rabies), then a list of the days and times at which the vets will appear in each village.

Rabies Day is a great social occasion here, with everyone and their dog congregating by the bus stop so that it is quite impossible for traffic to move in or out of the village for a couple of hours. The vet is there in his white coat and trilby hat, brandishing a high-powered pressurized syringe, while his assistant deals with the paperwork and tries to control the milling crowd. None of the animals appears at all upset, and our own mutt is usually so busy meeting and greeting that she has never yet noticed the injections.

The charge for this very important service is less than a pound, in exchange for which you get a bit of paper to keep among all the other bits of Portuguese paper, and which should be produced at the next year's round-up.

If you are bringing animals, talk to your own vet about items to keep in the medicine cabinet in case of emergencies. One of the unpleasant hazards in rural areas is the rat-poison that farmers sometimes put down and which all too often gets eaten by dogs. Your vet can probably recommend a quick-acting emetic, so that you can administer first-aid.

The Portuguese are mad about birds, and every little cottage has a cageful of canaries or budgerigars. We have not yet found a local vet who is much good with birds, but you may be luckier. If any of ours look under the weather, the pet shop proprietor usually has an effective remedy.

12. Paying Your Way

The Portuguese do not seem to believe in mailing bills. Not in this part of the country, at any rate.

Water and electricity bills are very often presented by hand, and that hand remains outstretched until the money is passed over. If there is nobody home when the bill is due, it is left in the mailbox, and the recipient then has the responsibility of paying up within the specified time—which is usually only a matter of a very few days.

This can sometimes be a trial.

In our early days, if the apartment was empty when the water man came with the monthly bill, it cost us something like £1.50 to drive to the town hall to settle an account that was quite often less than 35 pence. Which was irritating and a great waste of time. (Don't get too excited at the idea of paying such a tiny amount for a month's water. Over the year, our monthly bill averages out at a great deal more than 35 pence. Every so often and when we least expect it, we get a gigantic *factura* for no reason that we can see or that the water man can explain.)

There is, so we're told, an arrangement whereby you can get a form from the *Câmara* which will enable the bank to pay your debt to the municipality—out of your account, of course. But it seems easier in our case to leave an envelope marked, probably inaccurately, "*Exmo. Sr. de Agua*", stuck on the door with the money, or to make an arrangement with a neighbour.

It is as well to pay any utility bill on the dot, however inconvenient it may be. For a country where time is not necessarily of the essence, the Portuguese are remarkably stern about payment for water, electricity and telephone, and you can find services cut off with amazing alacrity. Which is bad enough, but it can often take weeks to get it restored.

Be prepared for muddles over foreign names.

Shortly after we moved into the apartment and before we had even met our local water man, we received a fierce, red-printed Final Notice which made it very clear, even without a dictionary, that we had two days in which to pay our outstanding bill, otherwise we would be waterless. There was no mention of the sum involved, but we feared the worst.

Armed with cash, cheque books and our large, useless dictionary, we hastened to the county town and the *Câmara*, where we had already been warned that nobody spoke English. Two and a half hours later we were still waiting by the counter while two clerks waded through foot-thick files and the lengthening queue behind us muttered quietly. Just as we were giving up hope there was a small squeak of triumph, a young man tore a sheet from a file and slapped it in front of us. We nearly fainted.

In five weeks, during which we had had long daily water cuts, we had apparently run up a bill of close to £300. There were all four of my husband's names neatly copperplated across the ledger—in Portugal, every name is always written out in full on every official paper. We took another look and almost fainted again, this time with relief. Three of the four names, strangely, were my husband's but the fourth, the all-important surname, was a near miss and certainly not ours. Luckily we had passports to prove it.

Don't ever grumble about all the identification you are required to carry around with you in Portugal. You never know when it can come in extremely useful.

Electricity bills

In some areas, the man who comes to read the meter also returns with the bill. In others, when you pay one month's bill, either at the EDP office or at some specially appointed place (ours is the local bakery), you collect your coming month's bill as you get the current one receipted.

Which is not to say that your meter has necessarily been read. There is a certain amount of guesswork involved in the assessment of consumption, but it all evens out in the end. Outside the greater Lisbon area, if the reader can't get at your meter he or she will leave a yellow card which you are supposed to fill in with the meter reading, sign, date and send to the office. You will see a space for your registered number and you write the figures that appear on your meter alongside the letter D.

In Lisbon, it is far more simple. Since the beginning of this year, consumers have been able to phone in their meter readings on a regular basis. This means that they pay the proper amount each month, rather than the minimum rate as long as their meter goes unread. The number to call is 672061.

Telephone and television

The telephone bill, as you know, used to be delivered by the postman and paid on the spot. That has now changed. But unless the post office also changes its accounting system, the monthly phone bill will probably cause some harsh words.

As things stand at the moment, it is impossible to sort out a phone bill because the calls are not now itemized. They used to be, before direct-dialling was introduced, but not any more. There is the standing monthly charge, which will almost certainly have gone up from the 1987 figure of 1,155 escudos; then three other kinds of charges—those for the calls you dialled directly both in and out of Portugal, those calls that went through an operator, and charges for any telegrams you were brave enough to send by phone.

When calls to Britain and other countries were placed through the International Operator, they took ten times as long, but they were listed on your bill. Which, if nothing else, gave you a small leg to stand on if you wanted to argue that bill.

But even in those days, the dictum was Pay Now, Argue Later—and that has not changed. It is no use getting tough and withholding payment while you discuss the matter. Your phone will probably be cut off and it may be weeks before you get it back. It is easier on the nervous system to convince yourself that what you lose on the swings you will eventually gain on the roundabouts. Whether any adjustments really are made, I don't know, but we have found that an outrageously high bill one month is quite often followed by a suspiciously small one the next and, not having the courage of our Portuguese, we tend to leave well alone and trust that the swings and roundabouts will do their stuff.

The monthly bill now comes by mail and can be paid the same way, within two weeks. Or it can be paid at any post office. Send or take the whole bill and part will be receipted and returned to you.

The annual (or semi-annual, if you prefer) television licence is also paid at the post office, and if you have bought your set in Portugal and registered it (see Chapter 3), the notifications will come through the mail. Take the form and your money to the appropriate post office wicket. In 1987 we paid just under £11 for a year's black-and-white viewing; people with colour sets paid twice that amount. If you brought your TV from Britain or acquired a secondhand one here, keep an eye open for announcements on television about tax-paying time (*Fiscalização de Taxas*) in specified areas.

Cash in hand

The only other local bill we get in the post is the one from our insurance agent. We could, of course, put a cheque in the mail, but we have become so accustomed to the personal approach that we automatically trot into town to hand over the money. It seems friendlier, somehow.

Unless you are the one who is sending out the bills. Then this nice friendly system loses some of its charm. Faced, a few years ago, with the prospect of trudging around the neighbourhood trying to collect payment from fifty or sixty advertisers in a small local paper, we lost some of our enthusiasm for the Portuguese way of doing things.

Tax payments

If you own property in Portugal or you earn an income here, you will of course pay taxes. And you are expected to know when those taxes fall due, which means paying attention to press and television because you get no notification through the mail. (See page 230.) You don't even get the tax forms, as we did in Canada. These have to be collected from the local tax office. Until you get used to these horribly complicated forms, you would be wise to find someone qualified to help you. An accountant's fees are very small beer compared with the anguish of trying to find your way around their complexities.

For the ordinary property-owning, income-earning foreigner living in Portugal, the first bout of tax-paying comes in January with the *Imposto Profissional*, a personal tax on all money earned in this country during the previous calendar year. It makes no difference how that money is earned. Doctors, bar-tenders, bricklayers, baby-sitters, people who rent out rooms, charter their boats or do any kind of part-time work are all expected to pay up.

There is a tax-free figure which amounts to fourteen times the current minimum wage. In 1986, that wage was 17,500 escudos a month, which gave every earner 245,000 tax-free escudos, or roughly £1,167. After that, the tax was assessed on a sliding scale up to 20.5 per cent.

If, as a resident, you have an interest-earning deposit account with a Portuguese bank, you do not have to include that interest in your tax return. It is deducted at source by the bank.

When the *Imposto Profissional* forms have been completed, preferably by an expert, take them to the Treasury Section of the *Secção de Finanças* (the local tax office) with the money. If you are giving a cheque in payment, the amount must be written in Portuguese and not in English.

Also payable in January is half of your *Contribuição Predial*, the Portuguese property tax which, like British rates, is based on the rentable value of your house or apartment. There are different schedules for urban and rural properties, but the final bill will almost certainly be a tiny fraction of the rates you have been paying in Britain. Most people pay their *Contribuição Predial* in two whacks, one in January and the other in July. But it is possible to apply for permission to make quarterly payments in January, April, July and October.

There is another personal tax to be paid: *Imposto Complementar*, which must be filed in June or July but is not payable until October. Some time in September you will receive notification through the mail, saying how much you have to pay.

This tax applies to the joint family income from all sources.

Your local Tax Inspector in Britain will have told you all about the double-taxation agreement between the UK and Portugal, under which you can pay Portuguese tax rather than British on income received from the UK. Pensions, royalties, dividends on British investments and so on should be declared on your *Imposto Complementar* return, as well as any money you earned in this country. There are a number of deductable expenses, including child allowances, and all receipts must be produced.

When everything that can be deducted has been deducted, tax starts at 4.8 per cent for single people and four per cent for those who are married. Maximum tax payable is sixty per cent for singles and fifty per cent for married couples.

If you file your returns late, you are fined.

Last year we had not been paying attention to the tax-paying calendar (see page 230) and were at least two months late with our *Imposto Complementar*. In fact, we would have been even later had we not happened to be in the local *Secção de Finanças* on some other matter and been asked, quite casually, whether we had paid up. Horrors. And red faces.

We were sent across the hall to collect the necessary forms, whereupon the kindly official filled them in for us and explained that he was sorry about the 500 escudos fine. We paid gladly and parted the best of friends, with no hard feelings and cries of 'See you in January'.

It would certainly have cost us 500 escudos to have the two forms filled in by an accountant.

Incidentally, if you receive a sudden freelance sort of payment from Britain—if you sit in the Portuguese sun and write one of those BBC short stories, for example—payment may be held up while you complete a form from the Inspector of Foreign Dividends (Lynwood Road, Thames Ditton, Surrey KT7 0DP) and have it stamped by your local Portuguese tax office before returning it to Thames Ditton. When the money arrives, you should declare it on your *Imposto Complementar*.

Unless Portugal has managed to fight herself back into the black by the time you get here, be prepared for occasional kitty-replenishing taxes. One was announced out of the blue towards the end of 1983. What they very rightly called an

Extraordinary Tax that caught everyone by surprise and, sadly, affected quite a few Christmases. It was, Prime Minister Soares said, an emergency measure, and it worked out at about six per cent of earned income.

At the risk of boring by repetition: all these figures will probably increase. Even so, if you are used to paying British taxes, the Portuguese ones will be no hardship and, in terms of what you receive in return, a very good bargain.

As in Britain, you pay no Capital Gains Tax (*Imposto de Mais Valias*) if you sell your Portuguese home. Here, Capital Gains is purely a business tax—at the moment.

But *Imposto de Sucessões de Doacões*, Death Duties, apply to everyone who leaves an estate in this country. And if that estate is a large one by Portuguese standards, the heirs may have a hefty bill. A great deal depends on who those heirs are. If the estate is small and the beneficiaries are the immediate family—spouse and children—there may be no tax to pay. But the larger the legacy and the further removed the beneficiary, the worse it gets. If a friend who is no blood relation inherits a few million escudos from you, he can pay up to seventy-five per cent in tax.

There are a number of taxes, other than IVA, that are payable by companies rather than individuals. The federal and municipal ones, those that have to do with importing and so on. And another Extraordinary Tax that has apparently become a permanent fixture, adding another five per cent to the Industrial Tax. You don't need to know about these at this stage and, by the time you get to Portugal, the details may well have changed. If you are proposing to go into any sort of business here, you will need an accountant to guide you through the commercial maze. The British Embassy in Lisbon will give you a list of Portuguese accountants who presumably speak English.

Day-to-day payments

These are made either in cash or by cheque. Private individuals, certainly in this area, do not run monthly accounts with shops as they do in Britain. Though in the smaller communities purchases can go "on the slate" by friendly agreement, it takes a little time to establish that kind of neighbourhood credit.

In Lisbon, Oporto and the tourist areas there are shops and restaurants that will accept the better-known credit cards, but so far there are no credit card facilities for the purchase of petrol or oil at filling stations.

Credit buying, other than the informal variety, is not anything like as rampant as it is in North America and Britain. It is certainly not publicized to any great extent, and there is no Portuguese equivalent of the blood-sucking North American finance company. If you are buying something expensive like a car or a houseful of furniture, you may be able to come to some private agreement with the seller.

If you were buying a car, for example, you could probably make a down-payment of twenty-five per cent of the purchase price and agree to pay the balance, plus interest, in thirty-six monthly instalments. You would then sign thirty-six *letras* (promissory notes) which the dealer would discount at his bank. For the next three years you make your monthly car payments to the bank.

Which brings us to the subject of:

Portuguese banks
As you probably know from holidays here, the banks in this country can function considerably more slowly than the mills of God. In the height of the holiday season, it can take an unconscionable time to cash a simple traveller's cheque, and it seems as though every bit of paper must be scrutinized by at least three different people before you get your money.

It gets marginally better once you have acquired your *Autorização de Residência* and a non-tourist bank account. At least you are no longer sentenced to stand in line for hours surrounded by half-naked oily bodies. But it is still a slow process.

Once again, it is pointless to grumble. It takes time to bank in Portugal, and that is all there is to it. Once you have deliberately erased everything you were accustomed to in your friendly neighbourhood Nat West and geared yourself down to the Portuguese way, you will become cheerfully acclimatized. And probably as annoyed as the rest of us to hear loud foreign voices explaining how a Portuguese bank should be run.

As soon as you have your *Autorização de Residência*, you are entitled to open as many bank accounts as you wish, and to feed them with escudos, sterling, dollars or whatever you have handy. Large capital sums of foreign money, though, should not be imported without a licence from the Bank of Portugal —ask your bank manager about it.

Until you are well known in your local bank, it will probably take three or four weeks for a foreign cheque to be cleared and appear as a deposit in your account.

To open a bank account and unless you want to discuss it first with the manager, ask at the wicket labelled *Expediente* and you will be given forms for a joint or an individual current or deposit account. You need to hand over some money, of course, and quite a substantial amount in the case of a deposit account.

If it is to be a joint account and you are blessed with a whole string of Christian names, the cheques will most likely be printed with the husband's name only, simply for lack of space. But the account will still be registered as a joint one.

It will probably take a couple of weeks before you can collect your new printed cheques—not bound into a cheque book but loose, stubless and slipped into a plastic folder. Forty escudos will be debited from your account to pay for this. Records of cheques issued are kept on a separate piece of ruled paper, and you had better practise small handwriting because there is never enough room to get everything in.

Portuguese cheques are made out differently to the ones you are accustomed to. The essential components are all there: date, payee, amount in both figures and words, your signature, but they are all arranged differently (see page 231), and a Portuguese bank also wants to know where you are writing that particular cheque. A cheque can be crossed, to ensure that it goes straight into the payee's account. Simply draw two parallel lines across the face of the cheque.

It is permitted to write the amount of the cheque in English in almost all cases. However, if you are giving a cheque for something official, such as your tax, the amount must be written in Portuguese.

In most banks, every cheque-cashing exercise starts with that *Expediente* counter. Your cheque is taken, peered at, stamped and scribbled over before it is passed to one of the paying-out people. In exchange you get a numbered plastic token. You then join the crowd and hang about practising your number in Portuguese so you will recognize it when it is eventually called. Don't expect people to stand in orderly queues, as they do in Britain. The Portuguese don't go much for queues, in banks or at bus stops. They prefer to collect in groups for a nice chat. British tourists always find this very strange.

Depositing a cheque is usually quicker but more intimidating, because the forms make little sense at the beginning. (See page 232.) Again, look for the sign above the counter: *Depósitos*. If the clerk is not busy and if you can look gormlessly foreign and helpless, he or she will sometimes take pity on you and do the necessary form-filling. In which case, hang on to the copy you get back and use it as a crib next time you go to deposit a cheque.

Bank statements arrive about a month after the date of the last entry and, though they are not too explicit and mention no names or details of transactions, they are easy enough to unravel because the issued cheque number appears in every case. Which is a great help, so long as you always remember to write the number on the record sheet every time you issue a cheque.

So far we have found only two small problems with the Portuguese banking system, and they both have to do with the business of balancing your cheque book.

If it is absolutely necessary to have one of your cancelled cheques back, allow plenty of time for this exercise. Cancelled cheques are not returned to you with your statement but are filed away in the bowels of the bank. Which is what often happens in Britain, so there is nothing strange about that. But a Portuguese bank does not file cancelled cheques under account numbers, as you might expect. They file them chronologically, according to the date on which the cheque was received from the payee's bank—and that might be anything from the

normal three or four days to three or four years from the date
that cheque was written. In Portugal there is no time limit during which a cheque must be cashed before it becomes invalid.

Then there is the other problem. It is quite usual, for a
variety of reasons, to hand over or receive a cheque that has all
the necessary details except for the payee's name on it. Or,
instead of a name, to be made out to *Portador* (Bearer). In
either case, these unpersonalized cheques can do a lot of
mileage before they come to rest in the bank's vaults, because
they can be and very often are used as legal tender.

A friend of ours paid his cleaning lady's Christmas bonus
with a *Portador* cheque, because she had no bank account and
he had no cash in the house. She went off to buy festive fare at
her village shop and used the cheque in payment. The grocer,
in turn, passed the cheque along to settle a bill of his own—and
so it presumably went on. That was four years ago and as far as
anyone knows, that cheque is still travelling around Portugal.
It has certainly not yet shown up on our friend's bank
statement, and his cheque book is permanently out of kilter.

Pity the poor bank clerk who is asked to find a cancelled
cheque.

As in other civilized countries, it is a criminal offence to
write a cheque when you have insufficient funds to cover it. A
new law has recently been introduced requiring that all rubber
cheques are reported immediately to the Bank of Portugal and
to the local police. But the onus here is not entirely on the
writer of a bouncing cheque. If the payee does not present that
cheque within eight days from the date it was written, it is then
too late for the police to do anything, and the matter must go to
court if he wants to collect.

To anyone accustomed to up-to-the-minute, push-button
banking with bullet-proof windows between cashier and
client, this may all seem a little primitive and tedious. But you
soon discover the most advantageous times to do your banking
and even to enjoy the leisurely pace and the courteous
handshakes that conclude every transaction.

After Canada, where armed bank-robbery was becoming
the national sport where we lived, and gun-toting guards stood
around whenever money was being transferred, we were

delighted to watch a man shovel several million escudos into a bag, shake hands and saunter out of a Portuguese bank as though twice two didn't matter a bit. That was ten years ago. Now, sadly, we do get spasmodic outbursts of bank robbery in the larger cities. But compared with other countries where people keep money in banks, the incidence is very, very small.

One last word about banks. Not long ago, a new bill-paying system was introduced whereby telephone, water and electricity bills were automatically debited from the accounts of participating customers. In certain parts of Portugal, notably this one, the idea has not proved very popular, and quite a few people have had essential services severed because of what they insist was the bank's inefficiency. However, people who use the system here say it is improving.

Social security
Finally, if you employ a maid, cook, gardener or any other domestic help, you must make their monthly Social Security payments without fail.

There is a touch of the Alice in Wonderlands about this because, although you tell the *Caixa de Previdência* official how much you are paying your part-time maid, he or she will produce a completely different figure on which the *Caixa* contributions are assessed. The hourly rate for help in the house, according to the *Caixa* in this area, is currently 49 escudos an hour, on which the employer pays 14 escudos for every hour worked. The fact that the going rate is something well over 150 escudos an hour seems to be irrelevant.

There is of course a form to fill in and be presented with every monthly payment, and these come in a book (*Folha-Guia de Pagamento, Pessoal do Serviço Domestico*, which needs no translation).

Caixa payments can be mailed, if there is no Social Security office in your neighbourhood, and must be mailed if they amount to more than 500 escudos. Send your cheque to the *Centro Regional de Segurança Social* in the provincial capital and enclose two copies of the form, with a self-addressed stamped envelope so that one copy can be returned as your receipt.

13. Facts of Life

Though you have chosen to live in Portugal and are therefore subject to Portuguese law, this does not affect your status as a British citizen—assuming of course that you are a British citizen. When you leave Portugal for business or pleasure, you still travel on your British passport. If you marry in Portugal or become a parent, the British Consular people want to know about it so they in turn can inform the Registrar of such matters in the United Kingdom.

Your nearest British Consulate or the Consular Section of the Embassy in Lisbon is your link with the UK, and if you have problems that cannot otherwise be solved or questions that nobody else can answer, a consular official should be able to help.

As soon as you have settled here and have a permanent address, you should register the fact at the Consulate (see page 235). There is no great formality about this. All it involves is a trip to the office to introduce yourself, have your passport stamped and give the Consul or his representative your address.

All this may sound a bit pernickety now, many years after the Revolution, but in 1974 it was the Consul's responsibility to see that all British nationals living in his area could be moved quickly out of harm's way if the necessity arose. It did not, as it turned out, but the Consulate would still like to know how to get in touch with you in an emergency.

Much of a British consular official's life here is spent making out and stamping the various certificates that are needed to obtain the various Portuguese documents a foreign resident needs. Also in translating and notarizing documents, witnessing signatures and sorting out problems for Britishers whether they are resident here or simply holidaying in Portugal.

Soon after we got here, our son managed to get himself mugged and robbed in Lisbon—not, I hasten to add, by a Portuguese assailant but by a couple of foreign tourists. He did what any sensible person would do under those circumstances and went straight to the Embassy, hoping they would at least lend him a few escudos out of the consular kitty to get himself patched up and buy a bed for the night. No dice. But they did lend him a phone so he could contact us and explain why he was not halfway to Paris, as we had supposed. Only after we had driven at high speed to the nearest Algarve Consulate and deposited a stack of banknotes was he able to borrow an equivalent amount from the Embassy.

They are very reluctant to part with money, but a Consulate can get your passport renewed with quite startling rapidity. Before your current one expires, take it to the office with three passport photographs. Fill in the forms, pay the fee and you will get your new passport back from Lisbon within about a week. If you should lose your passport, report it to the Consulate immediately (and to the local police) and a replacement will be issued.

If you need to see the Consul on anything but a matter of extreme urgency, do him a favour and don't turn up at the office on a Monday. Consulates and the Embassy close at the weekends, and most Mondays are fully taken up with sorting out the various crises that have arisen on Saturday and Sunday: the tourists who have had car accidents, got themselves arrested or fallen ill.

Consulates charge for just about every service they render, except the routine registration stamp in your passport. Pasted up in the office you will usually find a large printed sheet listing the various fees—all quoted in sterling. But don't, as we once did, try to pay the Consulate in sterling. They want escudos, and rather more of them to the pound than the day's rate of exchange.

A Portuguese will

As mentioned earlier, one of the first things you should do when you get here is to have a Portuguese will drawn up. The

Consul can't do this, but he can very likely direct you to an English-speaking Portuguese lawyer.

Under Portuguese law, if a Portuguese national dies intestate, his assets are divided so that the remaining spouse gets one half of the estate, and the other half is divided between the spouse and any surviving children. If a British resident in Portugal dies without leaving a will, the estate is administered according to British law.

In either case and unless the estate is small, death duties (*Imposto de Sucessões e Doações*) have to be paid before anyone gets anything (see Chapter 12). A lawyer will be able to advise you how to arrange your affairs so that your beneficiaries will not be too badly bitten by the tax.

He will want to see your *Bilhete de Identidade* and your *Residência* and to know the full names of your parents and whether they are still living. (Just for once, nobody is much interested in where they were born.) If you have already made a simple English will, show him a copy and he will probably be able to make a similar one covering your Portuguese assets.

When the will is ready, it has to be signed before two witnesses, not in the lawyer's office but in a notary's office, probably the one in the local town hall or court house. It will be read out to you in Portuguese, so it might be wise to ensure that one of your witnesses is bilingual enough to do any translating. If you can manage the Portuguese yourself and you do not want to go chasing around after witnesses, you will very likely find that there are people on the premises who will perform this not very onerous duty. There are two elderly Portuguese gentlemen who hover around our local court house and who earn a nice little living witnessing things at 100 escudos or so a time.

Probate, says our Portuguese lawyer cheerfully, is not a lengthy business. But it is difficult to know what he considers lengthy. One foreign widower here has been waiting more than three years for his wife's estate to be sorted out.

Death certificates
A death must of course be registered at the *Registo Civil*, with a doctor's certificate stating the cause. If you need a British death

certificate for insurance purposes, the Consulate should also be informed. Otherwise, says the local Vice-Consul, it is not strictly necessary. However, it might help with the consular record-keeping, and besides, it seems only polite.

Burial in Portugal takes place very quickly, for obvious reasons, usually within twenty-four hours. There are undertakers in most large towns who are accustomed to making the necessary arrangements for foreigners.

Although this is a Roman Catholic country, there seems to be no problem about non-Catholics being buried in the local Algarve cemeteries, especially in places where there is a sizeable foreign population. If you find yourself in the unhappy position of having to arrange a funeral, be sure to choose a permanent resting place. In some Portuguese cemeteries there is a rather gruesome arrangement by which a grave may be occupied for only five years.

Space in the celebrated British Cemetery in Lisbon is becoming so limited that only those who were parishioners of one of the several Anglican churches or the United Church of Scotland in Lisbon, or of St Vincent's Anglican Church in the Algarve, may be buried there.

Cremation has been legal for several years, but it has only recently been possible. After an awkward hiatus, Portugal's only crematorium—the one in Lisbon—is now working again.

The next-of-kin may, of course, wish to have the body flown back to the UK for burial and the British Embassy warns that this can be extremely expensive. Several Portuguese undertakers say they can handle all the arrangements and one recently quoted a price of slightly under £2,000 for this service.

Many of the British population in this part of the country have left letters with the Chaplain of St Vincent's Church (Rev. Canon Douglas Ward-Boddington, Casa Raquel, Bouliqueime, 8100 Loulé, telephone (089) 66720) giving the names and addresses of their next-of-kin, information about where their wills are to be found, where and how they wish to be buried, etc. This seems a very sensible idea.

Marriages

Unlike some Roman Catholic countries, civil marriages are performed in Portugal, as well as church ceremonies. If you are planning to marry here, you must notify the Consulate at least 21 days before the wedding date.

A British girl who marries a Portuguese national can make application for Portuguese nationality without having to give up her British one. Children of that marriage will also be entitled to dual nationality if they were born in Portugal, registered without delay at the British Consulate and entered on their mother's British passport.

Children born in Portugal to foreign parents who have lived in this country for six years and who do not work for a foreign organization may choose to take Portuguese nationality when they come of age. In the case of a boy, this would then mean that he is eligible for his stint of military service in one of the Portuguese armed forces. But this, judging by the lads in this village who have done or are doing their year-and-a-bit in uniform, seems to be no great hardship.

Before the Revolution, there was no such thing as divorce in Portugal. Now it is legal, and the grounds are much the same as they are in Britain.

A divorced person, British or Portuguese, wishing to re-marry here must produce copies of their previous marriage certificate and of the Decree Absolute stating the grounds for their divorce. These papers are sent to one of the four Portuguese Appeal Courts (in Lisbon, Oporto, Coimbra and Évora), and in due course permission will be granted by the *Tribunal de Relação* and the wedding can go ahead.

For a British couple living in the south of Portugal, one of the easiest ways to get married is to fly or drive to Gibraltar. There you can get married by special licence, in English and without having to establish any phoney residence. To do this, you need an affidavit sworn before the British Consul, giving names, addresses, dates of birth and, in the case of minors, written consent from parents or guardians. If either or both parties have been previously married, the original or a certified copy of the Decree Absolute is required. A widow or widower remarrying will need to show a copy of their spouse's death certificate and their previous marriage certificate. The Consul will tell you the current fee, which is then sent with all the necessary documents to the Registrar of Marriages, 30b Town Range, Gibraltar. When the Governor's Special Licence is issued in a few days' time, the date can be set. Take two witnesses with you and, of course, passports.

With any change of marital status, all your Portuguese documents have to be changed.

If a British national marries a Portuguese national in Great Britain, that marriage can be dissolved only in the UK and under British law. A British wife would, for example, have to go back to Britain and file there for divorce from her Portuguese husband.

A recent newspaper article here on the high rate of divorce in Portugal since it became lawful said that most cases were uncontested because of the huge legal costs. A local *advogado* said this was not necessarily so and quoted a figure that seemed extremely reasonable. The difficulty is, he said, that divorce is such a recent addition to the laws of Portugal that no fee structure has yet been laid down by the Portuguese Bar Association, or whoever lays these things down. Charges are made according to the amount of work done by the lawyer and ought, he said, to take also into account the financial situation of the clients.

Legal charges for any service do seem to vary enormously from one lawyer to another. The fee he quoted for handling a straightforward divorce case was precisely the amount we had paid another lawyer for drawing up a Power of Attorney.

Portuguese law
The law, like so many other aspects of life in Portugal, is changing at high speed and, as far as a foreigner can tell, for the better. Certainly where women are concerned.

Originally, Portuguese civil law was based on the Napoleonic Code under which, as we knew from bitter experience in French Canada, a married woman was nothing more than a chattel and had virtually no rights whatever. Until they de-Napoleonized Quebec's provincial laws, I could hardly breathe without my husband's written consent, and I could neither buy property nor go into business. When our small son needed an operation, I had to drag my husband out of a business meeting to sign the form admitting the baby to hospital, because I did not have the authority to do so.

Pre-Revolution Portugal must have been much the same until the early 1960s, when a few changes were made in the Civil Code. Many more were made after the Revolution, and now, as far as family matters are concerned, father and mother have equal rights and an equal say in the bringing up of their children. If they really cannot agree on some important point, the matter can be taken before the Family Court which is usually held at the local Court House.

Do try not to go to court about anything. With all these changes going on, it takes a good, conscientious lawyer twice the normal time to do his homework because the precedent he may be using can change overnight, making it necessary for him to do a great deal of checking and re-checking while his bill mounts up like a taxi meter. The courts are so jammed that it takes an incredible time to bring a civil action before a judge. And to make matters worse, that judge may not even turn up on the day you finally get a hearing.

There are cases, according to Portuguese law, that must be heard not by one judge but by three. Which means that an already overworked judge may suddenly get the call to go to another court and be part of a triumvirate. He has no choice but to leave his own court, perhaps for several days, during which his own overcrowded calendar gets set back even further.

If you should be arrested for anything more serious than failing the breathalyser test and find yourself in jail, you will be asked if you have a lawyer and, if so, whether you want to see him. If you have no lawyer, the authorities will appoint one to represent you, should you so wish. This is not quite a Dock Brief, since there are no legal eagles hanging hopefully around the court; and it is certainly not Legal Aid, because you will get a bill. But an *advogado* will be selected and instructed that he has a client. The only way he can avoid coming to see you and representing you is if he can prove a conflict of interests. If, for example, you are about to be charged with assault and the assaultee is already one of his clients.

Try not to get arrested over the weekend, when all the British Consular officials have gone home.

Police

The law in Portugal is enforced by several bodies, all of whom are armed, which you may find alarming at first.

The paramilitary GNR (*Guarda Nacional Repúblicana*) police the countryside in pairs on foot, horse or motor-bike, and in bunches in vans. They also set up road-blocks for reasons of their own.

For a long time we thought that the mounted GNR, who always seem to be picked as much for their good Latin looks as for their horsemanship, were riding along the Algarve roads to give female tourists a thrill. Nothing of the sort, of course, but they still look wonderfully decorative on their beautiful horses.

Every town has a GNR post and very probably a station where the *Policía de Segurança Publica*, the grey-uniformed city police, look after such matters as stamping those registration cards for visitors, fines for traffic offences, bouncing cheques, and articles that are lost, stolen and found—when they are not directing traffic in the town, telling people politely that they can't park there, or patrolling the streets to see that all is well.

The *Brigada de Trânsito* (Traffic Brigade) are the cops who chase after speeding cars, who stop drivers of patently unsafe vehicles or those with their seat-belts unbuckled. It is usually the *Brigada de Trânsito* or the GNR who turn up at the scene of an accident to take particulars, and in the busy summer season they are out in force on the roads and highways.

Then there is the *Guarda Fiscal*, the official body of what are ostensibly coastguards with a weather eye open for smugglers along Portugal's five-hundred-mile-long coastline. But in a small village like ours, the *Guardas* represent The Law.

If anything gets lost or stolen or strays, the matter must be reported at the *Posta*, the whitewashed building down on the beach where the national flag flies and melons are often put to ripen on the roof. Here, the duty officer will fill in all the necessary forms and make all the necessary phone calls. When a hopelessly inefficient burglar was spotted in the village a few years ago, the *Guarda* turned out in force, commandeering a passing Land Rover and giving chase. At the daily fish auction a *Guarda* is always present to oversee the pricing of the night's catch. And if there is a foreign-registered car or caravan in the neighbourhood for longer than the legal six months (see Chapter 8), you can bet your boots that a pair of our finest will appear on the doorstep to ask awkward questions about it.

14. Day-to-Day Living

It takes a while to become accustomed to the Portuguese pace and the Portuguese way of doing things. Ordinary, everyday things like getting shoes mended, paying the electricity bills, contacting a plumber or posting a parcel.

This may not be the case if you have chosen to live in a large city, but it is certainly so in the country areas and the less developed corners of the Algarve where facilities you have long taken for granted in your British home town may not yet exist: dry cleaners, laundromats, stamp machines and public telephones.

There were a few early days here, I must confess, when the sheer frustration of trying to buy something as simple as a bottle of ammonia or a mop could almost reduce me to tears, and the search for a two-way plug could take all morning. We would go hopefully into the town with a page-long shopping list and a dictionary, and count ourselves clever if we managed more than three items on that list. (Ammonia, should you ever need any, is sold here by a chemist—*farmácia*—and not by an ironmonger, as it was in Canada.)

Every little chore took for ever when we first came to live in Portugal. Partly because we did not speak the language. Partly because the shops in our local town were not nearly as well stocked as they are now. And partly because we had become so accustomed to the North American way of life that we found it difficult to change our ideas.

Especially our ideas about the value of time. Over there every minute of everyone's time carries an invisible dollar sign, and it would never occur to a lady behind a counter or cash register to keep a line of customers waiting while she chatted with a friend. Here, conversation can easily take precedence, and it is not the slightest use sighing, coughing, making excuse-me noises or even waving money under a Portuguese nose. It is rude to interrupt, and you simply have to wait it out, as the Portuguese do.

This cavalier attitude to time, though, does have its advantages.

Shortly after our television set was installed, we switched on one evening to find the screen entirely blank. Not even a flicker to show that somebody somewhere was trying to put things right. The following morning we reported the matter to the shop and were told that a technician would come out to the village that evening. We knew enough at that stage to be agreeably surprised when he turned up, as arranged, a few minutes before programming was due to start. We might also have known enough to expect a picture to appear the moment he switched on the set, just as a tooth stops aching as soon as you walk into a dentist's waiting room.

At what time had this breakdown occurred the night before?

At about half past seven.

Ah, that would explain it.

At seven o'clock the previous evening, the local transmitter had had some kind of technical accident, and television all over the province had been blacked out for four hours.

Greatly relieved but feeling more than a little silly, we asked for the bill. But he had done nothing. There was therefore no *factura*. But what about his time—at least an hour of it? And the drive from town and back again? *Não faz mal. Não problema.* No work, no bill. But since we had been kind enough to mention it, he would certainly accept a glass of wine before wishing us *boa noite*.

In 1978 in Canada that would have cost us at least $30. Heavens knows what the charge would be now.

As time is of such small consequence here, compared with Britain and North America, you can spend a lot of it hanging around waiting for people to deliver or come and mend things.

The only way to prevent rising blood pressure, we have found, is to take it for granted that the plumber who promises to come on Monday will not pitch up until Monday week at the earliest. If he comes on, or even near, the appointed day, it is a cause for celebration.

Household help

Living in a small Portuguese village, it soon became obvious that we should ask a local lady to come in once or twice a week for a few hours and help with the housework. Not only because I am an indifferent housekeeper but because it was more or less expected of foreigners. It is actually a very good idea, even if you can manage quite well on your own. You will probably learn more practical Portuguese from your maid than from any language course and, if you are lucky, she will be a friend, adviser and direct link with the local Portuguese people.

We have a love of a lady who comes at the most unexpected hours to restore a little order in this paper-ridden apartment and who could, I am sure, earn a much better living teaching Portuguese to foreigners. While she is chasing the dust and the birdseed, she chats away about the local goings-on, always alert for the blank-eyed look which means we have lost the thread. When that happens, she back-pedals and tries again, rephrasing rather than raising her voice, until we understand. Josélia speaks perfectly good English, but she will not do so when she is with us. We are going to learn Portuguese, if it is the last thing she does.

She is also an excellent cook and a great believer in the local herbal remedies for this and that. With her help, I now know how to peel a squid, cure a cold with a brew of *bela luisa* (a verbena-scented shrub) and turn a handful of chickpeas and a morsel of veal into a substantial supper for four. One day, when we have both got new glasses, she has promised to teach me to do the beautiful crochetwork that all the local ladies produce in their spare time.

In the British Embassy fact sheet that is given to new or prospective residents in Portugal, they tell you: "Even un-trained domestic help is difficult to find, and good servants are very scarce." That may be so in Lisbon, or if you are looking for a fully-fledged butler, but in the Algarve it is not too hard to find a local girl who will usually have been well trained in the arts of housekeeping by her mother. Portuguese houses are immaculately kept.

The hourly, daily, weekly or monthly wages for help around

the house will depend on where you are living. Here, the going rate at the moment is something under a pound an hour. In Lisbon, you might have to pay over £100 a month for a living-in cook, and provide her with accommodation, food and uniform. If you live in a tourist area, you may have a little more trouble finding a maid in the summer, because the best ones are snapped up by the people who manage and rent villas to tourists.

If you engage a maid, cook, gardener, children's nurse or butler, you are required to pay their contributions to the Social Security service (see Chapter 12).

Rules about holidays are clearly laid down. All full-time employees in Portugal are entitled to one month's paid holiday each year, and everyone gets a Christmas bonus (known as the Thirteenth Month) amounting to another month's pay. Nobody is expected to turn up for work on national and local holidays, of which there are a great number (see page 220).

Housekeeping
Even with someone to help with the chores, you will probably find housekeeping in Portugal a very different kettle of *peixe* to housekeeping at home. And I would guess that the more organized you were before, the longer it might take you to adjust, unless you have chosen to live in a city with dependable services. If you are going to live in an untouristy Algarve village, you may have to scrap many of your old time-and-trouble-saving routines, like the one big weekly shop and the menu-planning for a dinner party two weeks hence.

In Canada, with a large upright freezer in the basement and an equally large refrigerator in the kitchen, we never had to make more than one shopping expedition a week, and meals could be planned well in advance. If, as very occasionally happened, a winter storm wiped out the city's electricity, it was restored within hours.

In a small Portuguese apartment, life was not nearly so easy to start with. When we grumbled to the builder that he had left no space in the pint-sized kitchen for even the smallest refrigerator, he merely shrugged and suggested we keep it in the sitting-room, as many Portuguese do. Spurning that idea, we found a niche for a fridge in a hallway alcove and abandoned any grand ideas about freezers—which were expensive and hard to come by in 1978, before much frozen food had found its way down to this end of the Algarve. After three months of somewhat hysterical housekeeping and constant long-lasting power failures, we thought again and agreed that, though it might not win any awards for décor, a freezer in the hall was infinitely preferable to no freezer at all. We were sick of stepping out of the bedroom and into a lake of cold water. When the power went off at night, the fridge promptly defrosted itself and puddled all over the tiles. Apart from getting cold feet, we were also wasting a lot of food until we invested reluctantly in a small freezer. Now I can't imagine how we ever thought we could manage without one.

Even with a good stable supply of electricity, you will probably find that some food that could be refrigerated for days at home will not last long in Portugal. In Canada, bacon and ham could be refrigerated almost to infinity because they were packed with preservatives. Portuguese products are not and, if you are without a freezer, it is better to buy in small quantities.

In 1978 I think only two of the several *supermercados* in our nearby town had freezers. And coming from North America, where everything had been cleaned, homogenized and packaged within an inch of its life, we were fascinated by the contents of those big white cabinets. Unwrapped chunks of fish, poultry and unidentifiable meat, large open poly bags of vegetables, loaves of bread all lying around in heaps and gathering ice crystals. If you needed half a kilo of shelled peas, you simply helped yourself from the bag and tried not to collect too many handfuls of ice at the same time.

All that has changed now. In the last few years, several Portuguese companies have started marketing well-packaged food of all kinds, some of it pre-cooked and ready to be defrosted (or not, as the case may be) and heated. All manner of vegetables, poultry, fish, hamburgery things and Portuguese dishes such as stuffed squid, codfish cakes and the local versions of pizza are available almost everywhere.

To make life easier still, we now have any number of foreign

and Portuguese-run delicatessens where the food is not
necessarily cheap but is at least different.

Card-carrying gourmets may find life a little hard in the
Algarve, where it is often impossible to find essential *haute
cuisine* ingredients and where, compared with the glorious
Fortnumish shops of Lisbon, there is not a great deal of choice.
There is plenty of food about, of course, but it tends to get a
little monotonous, and there are times when you can't look
another pork chop in the eye.

Portugal has nothing to compare with the big British food
chains, and you could fit three of the Algarve's largest *supermercados* into a medium-sized Sainsbury's. The last time I was
in Britain, I became quite disoriented in our old home town
branch at the sight of what looked like an acre of assorted
cheeses. Not to mention half a mile of dairy products, tinned
foods, meats and everything else. Here you will probably see
only five or six different kinds of cheese in any one shop. Quite
often, none at all.

This is another Algarve hazard. Things vanish from the
shops, usually in the summer when the province is teeming
with tourists. The cause may be a spell of bad weather in the
north, which supplies a lot of food to this province. Fowl-pest
may have broken out somewhere. The trains or trucks may be
on strike. Some time ago, the abattoir vets went on strike, and
the local butchers had nothing to sell but those highly-
garlicked Portuguese sausages.

Milk is one of the more common casualties. Luckily, it is all
of the long-life variety which can last for three months without
refrigeration; so if you have the storage space, you need not get
caught short. By the way, don't ever be tempted to buy milk
from the picturesque vendor who goes round laden with large
churns either on his donkey-cart or on his motor-bike trailer.
The milk is certainly fresh and probably delicious, but the
chances are that it has not been pasteurized, and that is asking
for trouble unless you boil it.

Every town has its municipal market, some more adventurous than others. I know for instance that it is a waste of time
browsing in ours for anything very far out of the ordinary, and
if we get a sudden craving for fresh raspberries, we have to find

some valid excuse to drive almost forty kilometres (the price of petrol being what it is) to a bigger, better and more exciting market.

This is always a joyous outing and we come back laden with avocados, custard apples, gulls' eggs, corn cobs, tightly furled broccoli, crisp celery, country cheeses, home-cured ham—and at least a kilo of heavy-gauge clear plastic bags for freezing, which are better and so much cheaper than the rolls of perforated brand-name bags. Also, if we are lucky, we haul home a supply of *bofes*, a rather intimate and very nasty looking mess of beef or pork that we feed to the dog.

Food shopping here is not so much a matter of making a list as of seizing a basket and setting out to see what you can find.

Bulk-buying is another good housekeeping habit you may have to abandon, depending on where you have chosen to live. If you are moving from a British house to a Portuguese apartment, storage space may be a problem at first. And although it is possible to buy some items in catering packs, if you know where to shop, we have not yet found anything in the Algarve to compare with, say, Bejam's in Britain.

You may miss the bargain-hunting when you shop here. Prices may vary a little from store to store or town to town, but shops seldom make dramatic price-cuts to unload lines or to compete with other establishments. Around Christmas time one or two *supermercados* bring the price of drinks down, but we always feel this is more a gesture of goodwill towards men than a commercial ploy.

Buy Portuguese

Anything that is imported into Portugal is subject to tax and is therefore more expensive than the domestic product. Food included. But in this last year there has been a noticeable reduction in the price of food coming from other EEC countries. Not a huge reduction, but every little helps.

The Portuguese in the Algarve, being conservative people, are not much interested in exotica like Lyle's Golden Syrup, Earl Grey tea, Aunt Jemima's Pancake Mix or La Choy Chinese dishes in tins. They prefer dark molasses to golden syrup, coffee to any kind of tea and they would never dream of spending as much as £3.50 on a packaged pancake mix when they could do it themselves for pennies.

These and hundreds of other foreign foods are imported more for the tourist trade than anyone else. Holidaymakers confronted with shelf after shelf of brand names that mean nothing will automatically reach for the ones they know: Nestlé, Kellogg's, Campbell, Crosse & Blackwell. For one sunny fortnight—or even for a few weeks in winter—they do not mind paying over the odds for something that will taste precisely as they expect.

But for anyone living in Portugal, and especially if they do not have money to splash about, this is silly. The Portuguese brands are every bit as good and usually a great deal cheaper. If you can find a Portuguese-made version of whatever you are shopping for, do at least try it. By law, all the ingredients are now listed, just as they are in Britain, with the predominant ingredient at the top of the list.

Instead of paying ridiculous prices for Kellogg's Corn Flakes, try the ones labelled Nacional. And all the pasta products, biscuits and anything else made by the same large Portuguese company. Compal has an enormous line of tinned add-water-and-heat soups, which are as tasty and more interesting than the costlier ones made by Campbell. In the dried soup department, both Maggi and Knorr brands are made here, to suit Portuguese tastes. Locally made Tocafé is the equivalent of Nescafé, and Molho Inglêse peps up your Bloody Mary just as well as the expensive imported Lea & Perrins Worcestershire Sauce.

In the grocery freezers you will now find familiar brand names like McCain and Findus—who have just introduced the ubiquitous fish fingers into Portugal and whose hamburger patties are no thicker or better than the Portuguese ones sold under the Iglo label. They are just more expensive.

There is no doubt that in the last two or three years, even the Algarve grocery shelves and freezers have become much more interesting. Partly, presumably, because of the reduced taxes on foods from other EEC countries and because of the new influx of foreign companies into Portugal. And also because it looks, from a consumer's viewpoint, as though the

Portuguese food manufacturers are becoming much more enterprising.

Now, for the first time in our memory, we can buy boxes of tea-bags with good British names and flavour to match. A great improvement over the tasteless stuff we got before, the only alternative to those expensive tins. There is a larger selection of pet foods, Portuguese-made and also imported from Britain and France. They're still pretty costly, compared to people food and I boggle a bit when I have to pay out more than a pound for a tin of Chum—for a dog whose idea of a good meal are the very old fish-heads she finds on the beach.

Food and drink

Anyone who has been on holiday in Portugal knows that the fish is superlative and the meat can be less so. Especially the beef, which must be better in Lisbon than it is in the Algarve because so many of our restaurant-owners go all the way to the capital to buy their steaks.

The Portuguese, who eat ten times as much fish as they do meat, go mostly for pork, and looking through a list of the regional specialities, they appear to eat everything except the bristles. In the north, pigs' ears are grilled over charcoal or cooked with white beans. In the Alentejo they serve pork with shellfish, and trotters cooked with coriander leaves. They do wonderful things with pork liver, interesting and probably delicious things with bits of pig that do not bear thinking about. Very thrifty cooks, the Portuguese.

A Portuguese butcher's counter is not a pretty sight, with disembodied heads and suckling pigs staring reproachfully at you and great slabs of unidentifiable meat spread all over the place. But you soon get used to it.

Mutton is seldom seen, but you can buy lamb now and again. Kid, if you can bear the thought. Veal, which can sometimes look as pink as pork. The scraggy little yellow-skinned chickens that seem so unpromising are bursting with flavour, however you cook them. Duck, sometimes fresh but more often frozen; rabbit in season. Quail can usually be bought all year round.

A *bife* is a steak and may be of beef (*vaca*), pork (*porco*), tunny (*atum*), veal (*vitela*) or turkey (*peru*). We met a holi-daying friend in town one day, full of excitement because he had found, he thought, genuine imported Peruvian beef. We had to tell him gently that what he had actually found were slices of turkey breast. Turkey is one of the great standbys in the Algarve. Not a whole turkey, except at Christmas or by special order, but bits of bird: legs, giblets, wings and *bifes*.

All meat is expensive, now that the government has removed the price controls, and visitors say that Portuguese prices are much the same as they are in Britain.

Fish is not as cheap as it was, either. And I would suspect that the Portuguese no longer eat a per capita average of a hundred pounds of *bacalhau* every year. These days, the dried salt cod from the Newfoundland Grand Banks that used to be the staple dish costs more than a pound a pound, which is a lot of money here. But there are plenty of other fish. They say that more than two hundred varieties are sold in the Portuguese markets, and though we do not get anything like that number in our local *mercado*, there is usually an incredible selection on display. Some are familiar. Sardines, naturally, and iridescent mackerel, sole (or maybe flounder) of assorted sizes, skate, bass, bream, red and grey mullet, octopus and squid. All straight off the boat and so fresh that some of the poor things are still flapping.

On a good day there will be plenty of shellfish. The huge succulent shrimps that would be prawns in Britain, lan-goustine, spider crabs, little black and red crabs, cockles, clams—and some ferocious-looking things in shells, including a mammoth barnacle that is very highly regarded in these parts. Lobsters seldom get as far as the market here. They are snapped up by the restaurateurs almost as soon as they land on the beach.

Very occasionally we get tunny in the *mercado*, and that is quite a sight if you are only used to seeing tunny-fish tucked neatly into a tin. A monster of a fish, with a head the size of our dining table and brown, meaty flesh. A tunny steak braised with onions and tomatoes, Portuguese-style, has no fishy taste and can pass for the tenderest beef.

There are also creatures that I would not dare to buy and

would not know what to do with if somebody gave me one. Huge spotted pythons which I presume are eels, fish that are covered in spikes, others that seem to be all head. And the yards-long scabbard fish that look like strips of tinfoil. As a matter of fact, I do know what to do with those. You just cut them into diagonal slices and grill them—they are delicious.

If you live any distance from a town with a market, your village will almost certainly be served by the travelling vendors who turn up regularly bearing fish, bread, fruit and vegetables.

Even here, twelve kilometres or so from the town, the fish-lady arrives every morning with the back of her car packed with boxes of sardines, sardine-sized *carapau* (which I have often seen translated as stickleback but are more likely horse-mackerel) and a reasonable selection from the sheds where the night's catch has been auctioned. She starts leaning on the horn about a kilometre out of the village, and by the time she has parked at the bus-stop, the customers are there and waiting with their plastic bags.

The fruit and vegetable sellers bring their wares in by cart or motor-bike from the farms and nearby market gardens, to supply the village shops and anyone else who wants to buy. The bread van, too, since we have no village bakery. And half a dozen sellers of shoes, plants, sweaters, handicrafts, kitchen utensils and linens, who set up their stalls and unload their vans. By the time everyone has parked at the top of the village to do business with residents and tourists, it is a wonder there is any room left for the morning bus to stop and pick up its passengers, never mind move on its way. It is a tight squeeze, but somehow the driver manages to make it—with lots of advice from the onlookers.

As I've said before, if you are coming to live in the Algarve or any other popular resort area, be prepared for the local shops to run short of everything in the high summer season and for food shopping to take even longer than usual. The markets are packed with seething, sweating humanity by about nine o'clock, and shopping goes rapidly downhill from then on.

All the same, we were quite shocked to hear a British resident complaining in the supermarket about the hell of housekeeping in the tourist season. "They buy everything," she shrieked. "No wonder the prices keep going up"—which had to be one of the great *non sequiturs* of all time. And rude with it, since the supermarket was full of happy holiday-makers, exclaiming over the bargains and spending their nice foreign currency.

Catering in the summer can be a trial, but it does become easier every year as the Algarve towns grow larger and more shops open. And as you get more cunning about where and when you go to buy things. In sophisticated places like Lisbon and Oporto the business of day-to-day living is easier—but probably not so much fun as it is in the Algarve, once you get the hang of it.

Prices seems to shoot up every week, with marked increases whenever there is a rise in the price of petrol, which immediately affects the price of everything that is transported. It is hard on those with a Portuguese income, easier for the people with sterling or dollars because the slow devaluation of the escudo softens the blow.

However, it is by no means all doom and gloom. Far from it. Though the price of everyday food has doubled, tripled and in some cases more than quadrupled since we arrived here, only a few escudos have been added to the price of local wine. We can still buy a litre of perfectly acceptable Algarve plonk for less than 35 pence, and some extremely pleasant Alentejo wine for about 50 pence. You can do a lot better than that, as Raymond Postgate points out in his scholarly book on the subject of Portuguese wines. Since the country runs on *vinho*—the lunch baskets that workers carry are neatly designed to hold a litre bottle—the cost of even the most lordly vintage is, in British terms, a magnificent bargain.

One great benefit of EEC membership is that the price of whisky has come down. Pre-1986, recognizable Scotch was prohibitively expensive and confirmed whisky-drinkers either had to commit a large part of the housekeeping budget to their hobby, or else develop a more economical taste for one of the several spirits made in Portugal: gin, rum, vodka and brandy. Now the domestic liquor prices have suddenly gone soaring, but you can buy a 75cl bottle of whisky for more or less the same price as you would expect to pay in Britain.

Prices

There seems little point in making a long list of the current food prices. By the time you read this, they will be hopelessly out of date. Perhaps the easiest way to give an idea of the effect of both inflation and the shifting exchange rate is to list the contents of two shopping baskets.

In the summer of 1984 we spent 1,764 escudos in the village shop (£9.19 at 192 escudos to the pound) and brought back:

500g minced beef	700g fresh green beans
150g tomato concentrate	250g lard
250g margarine	250g butter
250g ground coffee	Medium-sized lettuce
100g Danish blue cheese	500g chicken giblets
2 rolls loo paper	3 apples
3 oranges	3 huge bananas
40 king-sized cigarettes	600g onions
2 litres local wine	Bunch of parsley
2 tins imported cat food	

In January 1987 we spent the same 1,764 escudos (now £8.40, with 210 escudos to the pound) at the same shop, and came home with:

250g Portuguese cheese	200g cheese biscuits
1 large tomato	2 garlic buds
1 litre local wine	1kg turkey wings
500g frozen peas	1kg onions
250g ground coffee	250g butter
1 apple	1 tin imported cat food

It was impossible to duplicate that first list in the depths of winter because some of the items were not to be seen and others, like fresh green beans at £1.50 a pound, were not to be bought—even in the interests of research. But had it been possible, it would have cost at least 3,000 escudos (£14.28).

The cost of living

Almost everyone we meet on holiday here wants to know what it costs to live in Portugal. It is a difficult question to answer because there are so many factors to take into account. Apart from the food which seems to occupy so much of one's thought, time and energy, there are the other family expenditures: clothing, wages, the annual rates and taxes, petrol and other car costs, medical expenses, insurance and heating.

If I seem to be harping on heating, it is because warmth is on everyone's mind at the moment—both resident and tourist —as we grumble our way through the worst of the mercifully short Algarve winter. After months of continuous sun and warm weather, the winter rains and sudden chilly spells come as a shock to the spoiled Algarveans. Some form of winter heating is essential, wherever you live. And unless you have bought or built a house with a fireplace and/or a central heating system of some sort, you will have to consider the relative merits and costs of keeping warm with the help of electricity, bottled gas, paraffin or a combination thereof.

Electricity, where available, is expensive and in some areas unreliable. But there are electric heaters of all kinds on the market here, from the oil-fired Dimplex type to the efficient (but expensive to run) blow-heaters.

Gas, butane and propane, is not very cheap either but it is easily obtainable since almost everyone uses it for cooking. It comes in 13 kilogram and 45 kilogram canisters, at slightly over 70 escudos a kilogram—plus, when you sign a contract with the dealer and haul the first canister away, a deposit of 2,000 or 3,000 escudos to cover the cost of the container. Thereafter you pay only for the gas, and your deposit is returned if you terminate the contract with that dealer. Gas heaters also come in several models, one of the most popular being the three-panelled kind that houses a thirteen kilogram bottle of butane at the back. With just one of the three panels burning, that bottle should last for about seventy hours.

Paraffin stoves are the least expensive form of heating, other than an open fire, but they are inclined to be a bit smelly. *Petróleo* is bought at filling stations and ironmongers, and, if you have safe storage, it is wise to buy a largish quantities because it can sometimes become scarce in winter.

There is one other thing that may or may not enter into your household budgeting: eating out in restaurants.

People on holiday are amazed at how inexpensive the Portuguese restaurants can be, compared with those in Britain, and we hear terrible stories about dinners for four back home that cost enough to keep a Portuguese family for a month. It is cheap here, especially if you patronize the small Portuguese restaurants that are geared to Portuguese pockets, and people eat out a great deal. A few years ago I think it was true to say that it could be cheaper to eat out than to dine at home. But prices have gone up, as they have everywhere, and these days I suspect only those who live pretty high on the hog at home can say that with any truth.

Two months ago, a pleasant but not particularly fancy dinner for four in a medium-priced local restaurant cost us £35. That included two bottles of wine, generous brandies with coffee and a rather enthusiastic tip. A main course in a run-of-the-mill restaurant costs around £4 at the moment, but less than that if you eat somewhere well off the tourist beat.

Dinner at home for the two of us, including wine, is under £2—unless we decide to egg-and-chip it, and then it is about 35 pence.

If we lived in Lisbon, we could probably afford to eat out more often. Restaurant prices are definitely lower there than they are in the Algarve.

I had hoped that, if I asked enough people for their ideas, it would be possible to produce a definitive cost-of-living figure. But of course it is not. No two families have the same priorities or spend their money in the same way. For some, a car is a major expenditure. Others give and go to plenty of parties. Some people make an annual trip back to Britain or take a long holiday every year. And there are those who have revamped their lifestyle so that they live almost as frugally as the Portuguese and appear to manage on practically nothing.

So much depends on where you choose to live and the things you are prepared to do without. The Portuguese authorities are not much help. A while ago they said that for people on holiday here the budget should be at least 1,500 escudos per person per day, excluding accommodation. Which works out at £428 a month for a couple, at the present rate of exchange.

With a house and car paid for, and depending on the area and way of life you have chosen, I would think a couple with no children to educate or animals to feed, and no great urge for a wild social life, could live simply but quite nicely on that holiday budget of more than £5,000 a year—five times the minimum wage in Portugal. And the consensus seems to be that it might be difficult, certainly for a middle-aged couple, to manage on very much less than £4,000 a year.

The only thing I can say with absolute certainty is that however much money you bring to Portugal, it will go further than it would in Britain.

15. Green Finger Exercises

Somebody once described Portugal as "The garden by the sea". Everything grows here, whether it is indigenous or not.

Next time you are in Coimbra, drive about thirty kilometres north-east into Buçaco National Park and the grounds of the Carmelite convent, where seventeenth-century monks planted a magnificent arboretum. You can count at least four hundred species of native-born trees and three hundred more that are foreigners, imported from India, Mexico and many other parts of the world.

While you are at it, if you are interested in matters botanical and in conservation, drive on up to the very north of Portugal, to the National Park at Peneda-Gerês. This region is so remote and its landscape so varied within the park's 193 square miles that you will find plants that have completely disappeared from the rest of Europe, destroyed by man in the pursuit of progress.

A great deal of Portugal is officially classified as having a sub-tropical climate, and north of the Monchique and Caldeirão mountains that border the Algarve it is also blessed with bountiful rivers and fertile soils. It seems that you only have to stuff a seed or a cutting into the ground and it flourishes.

Though the Algarve soils are fertile enough, gardening in the southern province is complicated by what can sometimes be acute water shortages. Through the long, hot summer there is seldom a drop of rain, and the province's annual rainfall is normally less than one third of the northern figure. None of which will prevent your having a glorious garden if you are coming to live in the Algarve. It just means a little more thought.

If you are taking over an established garden, you're lucky. All the hard work has already been done. If you are going to create an Eden out of the churned-up mess the builder left behind, you can start on the planning long before the last brick has been laid.

Soil and water
What type of soil have you got?

Along the Algarve coast it is usually sandy and quick drying, needing a good topsoil, with compost and manure. Inland, you are more likely to have acidy shale; or heavy clay and lime, with such poor drainage properties that by the end of an Algarve summer it can look and feel like pottery. In this case, you will need to add sand, manure and compost to make a good growing medium. Up in the mountains, the Monchique soil is definitely acid and will require some alkaline additive, unless you plan to grow nothing but rhododendrons, camellias and azaleas.

Soil-testing kits are available in the several Algarve garden centres, where you will also get expert advice on the problem of watering.

For a large expanse of garden, you may want to consider a sprinkler system. At the moment there are two types of manually operated systems on the Portuguese market: the conventional brass overhead kind and the pop-up. The first is splendid for shrubberies but a bit of a bore when it comes to lawn mowing because you have to mow around the installation and then tidy up with hand-clippers. The second type of sprinkler is more suitable for grassy areas because you can run the mower right over it. Better still is an automatic pop-up system which can be set to sprinkle at specific times, is built to cope with different soil conditions and will not get in the way of the lawn mower.

With only a small garden to tend, you may not need anything more elaborate than a garden tap, a length of hose and a volunteer to hold it.

Mains water can become chronically short in the Algarve summer months and, for anyone with a large, thirsty garden, very expensive. The ideal answer is to have a well on your property from which to pump unmetered water for your grounds; but this cannot always be arranged to order.

However, if you know anyone who dowses, it would certainly be worth asking them to criss-cross your property with their magic twig to see if there is an underground water supply. There very often is in this province, and a talented water-diviner can tell you not only the best place to bore but how deep you need to go. Around here water is usually found at about 60 metres and the going rate for well-digging is 5,000 escudos a metre. Which makes the cost of the average bore-hole, complete with pump, *cisterna* and all the bits, about £3,500.

A couple of relatively new arrivals in this neighbourhood are kicking themselves for not having thought of this before arranging and paying for municipal water to be piped about a quarter of a mile to their new house on the outskirts of a village. It cost them £2,500 to have water from the taps. Not long afterwards, they discovered that there was water on their land, only twenty-eight metres below the surface.

The one thing that is difficult to achieve in the Algarve is a velvety smooth Wimbledon-calibre lawn. Clubs and expensive developments manage it, but they have a staff of full-time gardeners to seed and pamper their lawns. What with the heat and the seasonal water shortages, most people settle for a lawn of coarse turfed grass. It may not look so elegantly English, but it is a whole lot easier to establish and maintain. Even during a rainy Algarve winter, it is still necessary to water your lawn if you want to keep it looking its best—and this also applies to lawns in any coastal area in Portugal. The warm sun and strong Atlantic winds combine to dry the surface soil very quickly, and a weekly watering of about 15mm is needed to keep the grass in good condition.

Privacy

A large garden may need a hedge around it. The attractive whitewashed walls that surround small Portuguese gardens are quite costly to build, and fencing is also expensive. A drystone wall is cheaper, providing you have settled in a rocky area where the material is easily available.

For a quick-growing hedge the garden specialists will probably recommend myoporum or cupressus lusitanica, both of which look very smart when they are clipped. For a flowering hedge you could plant melaleuca, escallonia, pyracantha or oleander. Be careful of oleander if there are going to be small children around, the kind that put things in their mouths, as oleander leaves are extremely poisonous.

If you want a windbreak to protect plants, bamboo is attractive, effective and fast-growing.

An Algarve garden
However small your garden, you will want a tree or two for shade, flowers or fruit. The sweet-smelling mimosa that costs so much in British florists' shops and that grows so luxuriantly along the Algarve roads needs very little water. Palms, well fed and watered, will grow surprisingly fast. Conifers, pepper trees, the early flowering jacaranda and Judas trees all prosper in this climate, as do magnolias and almost any fruit tree you care to mention.

No Algarve garden is complete without at least one citrus tree: orange, lemon, grapefruit, lime, tangerine. Peaches, pears, several varieties of apple, quince and pomegranate all do extremely well here; almond, olive and fig trees produce three of the province's major cash crops. A loquat tree is an attractive addition to a garden, producing a delicious fruit for jam and chutney-making.

Personally, I see no point in a Portuguese garden without grape vines. If you plant two-year-old vines against a wall or trellis, it will be at least two or three years before they produce much in the way of fruit, because it takes time to build the permanent branches. Grapes appear from buds on the previous summer's canes, and vines are pruned in late December or early January, before the sap begins to flow.

People who are not so addicted to gardening prefer to fill their plots with shrubs rather than annuals. Viburnum fragrans is a favourite in Portugal because it begins to bloom at Christmas and flowers all through the spring. Other popular plants that require minimum attention are the umpteen varieties of hibiscus, the multi-coloured lantana, cestrum, callistemon, cassia and datura.

In this part of Portugal, at any rate, you don't often see a wall or trellis that does not have something colourful clambering over it. Bougainvillaea, more often than not, in a riotous mixture of reds and purples; pink and white tecoma, flowering solandra, passion flower, begonia and morning glory with bigger and bluer flowers than you normally see in Britain.

Anything that grows in your British garden will grow beautifully in Portugal. Some may have to be planted with care, however. Pansies, for example, find the Algarve sun too strong for comfort and need to be placed in a shady spot. Roses relish it and bloom almost continuously here. Which is a great joy, but it means that the poor things get practically no rest period and therefore need to be pruned and fed throughout the year and not just cut back in the autumn as they are in Britain. If you cut the buds early, you'll find they last a lot longer in the house than they do in the garden, where roses tend to go blowsy within a couple of days.

The Algarve is great cactus country, and if your land is rocky outcrop, a collection of cacti and succulents will brighten up the landscape without consuming precious water. Ceraii and opuntias look very impressive, and opuntia monacantha gives lovely colour, blooming from May to December. Another good flowering variety is cereus peruvianus.

The tall yellow-flowered agave (century plant) is widely used to mark boundaries; mesembryanthemum is planted to counteract erosion. Prickly pears grow in gardens and along the roads, though nobody bothers about harvesting the fruit. Succulents such as sedum, echevaria, crassula and aeonium make decorative additions to rockeries and retaining walls.

Every Portuguese cottage has its vegetable patch. Tomatoes and *favas* (broad beans) mostly, closely followed by onions and peppers, cucumbers and, space permitting, pumpkins.

We were surprised one winter when our Portuguese neighbour presented us with a bag of small Brussels sprouts from her allotment. We had no idea she went in for anything so foreign. Other than the root vegetables which seem to be the staple winter diet here, we had seen only cauliflowers, giant cabbages and year-round New Zealand spinach on her plot of land.

It was the foreigners who started experimenting in the Algarve and producing novelties like sprouts, broccoli and courgettes, first for their own use and then for the markets. A British gardener introduced sweet corn in this area a few years ago; the British and other foreigners fell on it with shouts of joy, but the Portuguese were not impressed. They had been growing corn for generations, and feeding it to their animals.

The only vegetable that does not do particularly well in the south seems to be celery. You do sometimes see it in the local markets but, while the flavour is good, it is usually spindly green and a poor thing compared to the juicy white stalks one is used to in Britain. And nobody seems to bother about growing asparagus commercially here. Probably because it grows wild in the Algarve, as artichokes do; more likely because it involves a great deal of hard work and several years before that work is rewarded.

Cold spots

When you are planning your garden, watch out for frost-pockets. They occur even here, where frost is very infrequent, and in some low-lying areas the vegetation can be killed off overnight. The only way to find out about these death-traps is to ask the local people before you buy and plant dozens of orange trees.

And do take their word for it, otherwise you can end up with egg on your face. Like the man who recently invested heavily in what was going to be Portugal's first mainland pineapple farm. He had been a pineapple-grower in Africa and, despite what the villagers told him, his tests had proved conclusively that he had picked the perfect spot in the Algarve to grow his crop and make his fortune. Local people shook their heads and said he was *maluco* when he covered heaven knows how many hectares with expensively imported plants; and they felt so strongly about it that he had a hard time employing anyone to help him. When the frost came, his pineapples went. Fortunately, he had hedged his bet to a certain extent by growing a small proportion of his crop in plastic greenhouses.

Greenhouses in the south are more often made from heavy-duty plastic than from expensive glass; plastic cloches protect strawberries and seedlings from cold spells and pests. As the sun becomes hotter, ventilation holes are simply torn in the plastic sheeting, or it is rolled up to regulate the temperature. It looks a bit messy, but it is more economical and just as effective as the more conventional kind of greenhouse.

You'll find all the old familiar garden pests here and, if you don't want to bring a supply of antidotes, they are easily available from supermarkets and garden centres all over Portugal.

A word about snails in the Algarve. All through the summer, hedgerow and garden plants are encrusted with the wretched things, and though the thrushes and seagulls do their best, there seems to be an inexhaustible supply.

The garden that went with the house we borrowed when we first arrived was infested with snails, and the elderly gardener spent several hours a day bent like a croquet-hoop as he carefully picked them from fruit trees, walls and shrubs, dropping them into a plastic bucket. When he disappeared for lunch one day, we decided to lend a couple of hands. Ignorant hands, as it turned out, because we had no idea that the snails we prised from anything green and callously disposed of were a local delicacy. That bucket contained Afonso's lunch.

Algarve snails are, in fact, considered a rare treat in the Lisbon restaurants, and the men, women and children who scour the fields for them from May to October are earning a good summer living. A talented snail-picker can make more than 1,000 escudos a day during the season, and that's not to be sneezed at.

People say that a good gardener is as hard to find in Portugal as he is in Britain. But I suspect that if you let it be known that you would like some help, Portuguese word-of-mouth will eventually produce somebody's husband's brother's cousin who will come on a regular or *ad hoc* basis. The last we heard, the going rate in this area was around 300 escudos an hour for a part-time gardener. And more than that if your help comes through one of the several gardening services that have recently sprung up.

Some people around here have made mutually satisfactory arrangements about the growing and sale of fruit and vegetables. They take what they need from their garden, and the man who does most of the work sells the produce and takes the profit for himself.

Balcony and indoor gardening

Even if you are moving into an apartment, you can still keep your green fingers exercised. There is hardly a balcony in Portugal that is not filled with pot-plants that seem to flourish all year round. Indoors, too, the bright white walls of modern buildings provide plenty of light for plants.

There is one disadvantage to having an apartment with an unobstructed sea-view. When the winter winds come, they bring so much salt with them that windows become instantly opaque, and any plants on the balcony keel over. A row of open-work bricks along the top of the balcony wall gives quite good protection against the damaging winds and saves the bother of having to bring every pot indoors before the onset of winter.

Several species of pot-plant seem to survive the worst that seaside weather can do. Some of the hardier geraniums appear unmoved, bougainvillaea may take a beating but it recovers, and we have a particularly vicious sabre-leafed bromeliad of some kind with a spectacular red-and-blue flower which I greatly dislike and which I leave out all winter in the hope that it will quietly perish. It doesn't.

Six years ago, it was hard to find bags of earth for indoor plants. You took a trowel and went out to dig beneath the nearest carob tree. (You could dig wherever you liked, of course, but the Portuguese maintain that the soil around the protein-rich carob is the best.) Now you can buy bagged earth all over the place; also those useful peat-pots for seedlings, and the miniature greenhouse kits that help germination along. All these things have probably been available in Lisbon for years, but the Algarve is finally catching up.

16. The Pleasures of Portugal

"But what are you going to do all day?" our Canadian friends wanted to know. "Going from a city to a tiny village where you don't even speak the language, you'll be bored out of your minds."

They need not have worried.

For the first few months in Portugal we were—and you will be—busier than ever before. Getting over the move. Getting our bearings. Getting all the necessary Portuguese papers together. Getting used to the Portuguese way of doing things. Getting to know people. As a recent arrival remarked the other day in the pub, "I've been so damned busy ever since I retired here that I don't know how I ever found time to work in England."

A large part of one's early days seems to be spent asking for advice and information. Where do I find a maid? Where can I get the car serviced? May I use your telephone? Is there a plumber around here? What does this bit of paper mean? When we first came to this village, there were only four other English-speakers within earshot, and we were constantly on one or other of their doorsteps, bleating for help. It was always generously given.

It is wonderfully easy to get to know people in this part of the world. The traditional British inhibitions seem to wither away in the sun, and people who I am sure would never dream of talking to fellow-commuters on the 8.05 in real life are the first to make newcomers welcome. If there is a drawback to living in a predominantly Portuguese community, it is that you do tend to hear the same expatriate stories quite often and to go through your own repertoire more often than your husband or wife may think necessary.

It takes a little longer to get to know the Portuguese people.

They are friendly and kindly but not necessarily effusive about it, and they take their time about getting to know you. Not in any way standoffish, you understand, but just a little reserved. You are a foreigner and therefore a bit odd, but you are nevertheless made to feel welcome, and there is none of the resentment, overt or otherwise, that you so often feel in other countries. When friendship is offered, cherish it, for there is no better friend than a Portuguese.

When you have finally found your feet—and this may take longer than you expect—it might be wise to think about filling at least some of the long sunny days. If, of course, you have not already done so. The happiest expatriates we know are the ones for whom the days are too short to pack everything in. The least contented are the lotus-eaters, those who moved to Portugal with the idea of relaxing and letting the world go by, and are doing exactly that. You can lie on the beach or prop up a bar for just so long before terminal boredom sets in. And there is no excuse whatever for being bored in Portugal.

Getting together

If you are one of nature's joiners, there are plenty of clubs and associations, especially around Lisbon, where people of all nationalities get together for various reasons. Some are devoted to cheerful good works, others to hobbies, and still others to a little gentle flag-flying.

The British Legion has its principal Portuguese office in Estoril and branches in Oporto and Algarve. The Lisbon Women's Royal Voluntary Service is the only overseas branch of that splendid organization. Both welcome new members with open arms, especially if the members are prepared to work.

The Cheshire Homes people are active in Portugal, with one residential home in Carcavelos and another planned for Lagos in the Algarve. Funds, of course, are always needed. Fund-raisers with ideas, too, as well as people who are prepared to do practical jobs around the Carcavelos Home and to befriend those who live there.

The Charity Bridge Association combines business with

pleasure in Ericeira by arranging bridge tournaments in dozens of different locations, to help any number of organizations.

One of the most prestigious clubs in Lisbon is probably the Royal British Club which began in the 1880s as the Lisbon Athenaeum, a gathering of business and professional men. King Edward VII gave permission for the club to style itself Royal when it changed its name.

The Royal Society of St George shares the same premises as the Royal British Club, at Rua da Estrêla 8 in Lisbon.

Membership of St Andrew's Society is open to anyone with a Scottish grandparent and, as well as doing its share of fund-raising for worthy causes and organizing sporting events, the Society goes to town twice a year, on St Andrew's Day and Burns Night.

Exiled Welshmen will be glad to know that the St David's Society of Portugal pulls out all the leeks on 1 March every year and also arranges outings and get-togethers.

The American Women of Lisbon have a clubhouse in Cascais where all sorts of activities go on, from rug-making to bridge. This very friendly organization is not confined to ladies from the USA, luckily. If you speak English, you are eligible to join.

In Estoril, the Flower and Garden Club of Portugal welcomes visitors to its monthly meetings. And if you attended either university, you probably qualify to become a member of the Cambridge and Oxford Society in Estoril and to enjoy the twice-yearly luncheons.

Quite a few British and other residents are concerned with animal welfare in Portugal. At Quinta dos Cães, São Pedro de Sintra, volunteers look after and collect funds for canine waifs and strays. In the Algarve there are two such societies, both of which are constantly crying out for financial and practical help: the Lagos Animal Protection Society is one, and the other is the St Francis Dogs' Home near Loulé.

For theatre-buffs, the Lisbon Players have their own theatre where plays and other entertainments are staged regularly. The membership fee is very modest.

The British Council in Lisbon and in Oporto works with the Portuguese Ministry of Culture and the Gulbenkian

Foundation to produce a year-round programme of exhibitions, concerts, films and lectures in both cities. There are big annual music festivals in Sintra and Cascais, and those who like to sing should get in touch with the International Community Chorale in Cascais; this excellent amateur choir performs in churches, embassies and private houses, giving concerts in the spring and autumn.

In the Algarve
Because of the distances involved, clubbish activities are more difficult to organize in the southern province. Even so, there is currently a lot of chat about an amateur theatre group being formed, and by the time you read this, it may even have come to pass.

There are plenty of bridge tournaments in the large hotels along the coast. Bingo, too, since it has at last been legalized in Portugal. There is talk that they are going to turn one of the province's three very fancy casinos into an up-market bingo hall—to the horror of those who consider themselves above such things.

The Lions Club is active here, and the newly formed Lioness Clube do Algarve, who do a great deal of work for underprivileged Portuguese children. Rotarians meet regularly, and the Lagos Club is heavily involved in the building of the province's first (and Portugal's second) Cheshire Home.

Culturally speaking, the Algarve is at a disadvantage compared with Lisbon. But every summer we do have a two-month-long music festival, courtesy of the Ministry of Culture, the Secretary of State for Tourism and the beneficent Gulbenkian Foundation, with concerts, recitals and ballets by national and international performers who we would otherwise never see down here in the boondocks. In late summer we also have the annual National Folk Festival—a wonderful spectacle with dance groups from all over mainland Portugal and the islands performing around the Algarve.

So far, there is only one real cultural centre in the province, the one at São Lourenço, near Almansil. The Algarve Archaeological Association holds regular meetings there (and also in Portimão), and they have a full programme of music, art exhibitions, lectures and the like.

The closest we get to a non-sporting club in the Algarve is probably St Vincent's Church, an ecclesiastical oddity because, though the parish is large in souls, it has no church of its own. Services are held at different locations every Sunday of the month, and the peripatetic Chaplain divides his time between private houses, a school, a couple of restaurants and one interdenominational and one Roman Catholic church. This unwieldy arrangement does have its advantages, though, because the Algarve can have several Church Bazaars in the course of a year, and the local parish knees-up is always a great occasion. Everyone is roped in to run stalls, organize competitions, tend bars, cut sandwiches, man barbecues, sell raffle tickets, collect and sort donations, bake and make jams before the big day. And the foreign community turns out in force to replenish its bookshelves with battered paperbacks, stock up its gardens with potted donations, browse through the clothes stall and load themselves up with goodies from other people's kitchens. The proceeds, which are usually considerable, are divided between the Church and the local Portuguese charities, and a very good time is had by all.

But these are "foreign" activities and organizations. What about all the things that Portugal herself has to offer? There are dozens of different ways to pass the time in this country, especially if you are keen on sports.

Spectator sports
For those who enjoy watching other people rush around in the heat or risking their necks, there are plenty of spectator sports. *Futebol* is the national passion, and *Totobola*, the Portuguese football pools, is the national vice. Every village has its soccer team, and a boy from this one actually tried out for one of the English First Division teams. Sadly, he didn't quite make it, but we were all immensely proud of him.

Cars are raced around the Autodrome in Estoril and all over the Portuguese roads during the rallies, when everyone turns out to sit in the hedgerows and watch the competitors flash by. Cycle races also draw enormous crowds and are closely watched on television.

There are show-jumping competitions at Estoril, Cascais and Penina in the Algarve. Horse shows and dressage competitions at Mafra. Dog shows in Lisbon, Coimbra, Cacém and the Algarve. Plenty of golf tournaments, athletics meets and exhibition tennis in the larger centres.

And then there are the bullfights, which I refuse to discuss—except to say that the bull is not slaughtered before your very eyes, if that is any consolation to you or the bull.

Fishing

If fishing is your pleasure, you have come to the right place. Salt water, fresh water, rock, beach or underwater fishing —take your choice. Take the opportunity, too, to move away from your new home ground and see some of the rest of the country while you are enjoying your sport.

Freshwater fishermen, for example, should head north to the provinces of Minho and Trás-os-Montes, where the six great mountain ranges provide a network of rivers and streams, natural lakes and well-stocked *barragems* (reservoirs). There is fine sport to be had in central Portugal, which is also well-watered. The Algarve, however, is not—though you can fish the Bravura and Arade *barragems*, and you may have some luck in the Guadiana river. But generally speaking, the Algarveans do their fishing in or by the sea.

The freshwater season varies according to the species. You will need a licence from the local *Câmara*, where you will also get all the local regulations about the size and limit of your catch, and be told firmly that it is illegal to cast a line between sunset and sunrise.

For salmon fishing (1 March to 31 July), go up to the north-westerly rivers, the Minho and the Lima. Fishing of any kind is prohibited outside those dates in any waters where salmon are found, and you may not take salmon when they are returning to the sea after spawning.

The trout season also runs from 1 March to 31 July, and these too live in the Minho and Lima rivers. In addition, you will find trout in the streams and lakes of the beautiful Serra da Estrêla region.

One of the loveliest places for a trout-fishing holiday is on the edge of the Peneda-Gerês National Park, on the border with Spain. You cannot fish within the park boundaries because large parts of it are a nature reserve, but the *barragems* of Caniçada and Venda Nova lie just outside, as does a good stretch of the Lima. Both *barragems* are within easy reach of the Pousada de São Bento, just inside the park.

Carp and barbel (1 July to 14 March) are both found in the streams and rivers of central and southern Portugal. Fish for large-mouth bass (1 July to 14 March) in the Aqueda area north of Coimbra, on the Sorreia river between Coruche and Mora; in the Barragem do Meranhão, south-west of Portalegre; in the Sado river; around Elvas, in the reservoirs of the Beja region and in the Algarve. You will find shad (1 February to 14 July) in Portugal's rivers only during the spring. Otherwise they live in the sea and can be caught from the beach.

Experts say there is excellent fishing in the Tagus tributaries: between Abrantes and Castelo Branco, the *barragems* of Pracana and Póvoa. Further south, between Coruche and Portalegre, the Sorreia and Seda rivers offer good sport, as does the Barragem Salazar to the north-east of Alcácer do Sal in the Alentejo.

If you are thinking of fishing the Zézere river, between Tomar and Cambas, they recommend the reservoirs at Castelo do Bode, Bouça and Cabril; and on the Douro river, in the reservoirs of Miranda do Douro, Picote and Bemposta.

Several of Portugal's numerous health resorts—where people take the waters—also have fishing facilities, among others. There is a spa at Caldas do Gerês, in the national park, where you can give your liver a break while you do some fishing. Also in the north, on the fish-rich River Tâmega, there are spas at Chaves, Vidago and Pedras Salgadas. In the central area, Caldas da Rainha and Fonte Santa de Monfortinho have cure-and-cast facilities.

With more than five hundred miles of Atlantic coastline, not to mention between thirty and seventy miles of continental shelf, it is hardly surprising that most of Portugal's fishing goes on in salt water.

Those who know about such things reckon that this is one of the very best game-fishing countries in Europe, largely because of that continental shelf, which can go down to three hundred fathoms before it drops suddenly to more than ten times that depth. The shelf forms a convenient platter on which the small fish gather and from which the large ones come to feed.

You do not need a licence to go out for a day's game-fishing with the owner of a specially equipped boat. He already has all the necessary papers. All you need is a pocketful of money and a great deal of stamina. In the Algarve, a day's fishing costs in the region of 7,500 escudos, but in other areas, off the tourist track, it may be cheaper.

Most of Portugal's game-fishing goes on in the waters to the south of Peniche and along the Algarve coastline, where schools of tunny used to come comparatively close to shore on their way to the summer spawning grounds of the Mediterranean. Not so long ago, they were chased into a complicated maze of sturdy offshore nets at the east end of the coast, and slaughtered in their thousands before they could even reach the Med. Now, because the changing currents have made the shoreline too cold for these monster fish—and, I like to think, because they have grown smarter—the tunny make their journey eastwards further out to sea, in water too deep to set the nets, and the disgusting spectacle they called "The Bullfight of the Sea" is no more.

Sesimbra, on the Tróia peninsula close to Setúbal, is one of the big game-fishing centres. From here you can go out in search of shark, swordfish, conger, ray and tunny. In the south, Sagres is the most important centre, and in early summer tunny, shark and marlin are dragged triumphantly ashore to be photographed and lied about. Boats also go out from Lagos, Portimão, Faro, Tavira and other Algarve ports, taking tackle, bait, refreshment and everything else needed for a good day's sport.

The Portuguese do a lot of their uncommercial fishing from the beaches or, precariously, from the rocks. It is quite unnerving to see them perched part-way up the two-hundred-foot cliffs at Cape St Vincent, balancing on what looks like an inch-wide ledge and casting merrily into a gale-force wind. Only the most foolhardy foreigner or one with a good supply of Mohawk blood would try such a thing. But the Cape St Vincent fishermen go home on their motor-bikes, poles slung over their shoulders and a bag or basket crammed with bream, bass, mullet, mackerel and many more varieties of fish.

There is no need to be that macho. All along the southern coast there are other, less dangerous rocks to fish from. On the west coast there used to be good fishing at Sines, but that has been ruined by the new industrial development. And Ericeira, north of Lisbon, is the place to go in winter for bass and bream—if you can stand those cold Atlantic winds.

At various points along the coast you will see yellow signs on the clifftops, showing a leaping fish. These indicate the most popular areas, but you can fish wherever you like—or, more to the point, where a local angler recommends.

If you would rather not risk your neck, pick a likely spot and cast from the beach. Choose a cloudy day or, if the sky remains obstinately clear, go at sunrise or dusk to a stretch where there is some seaweeed or a few rocks. Cast for the spot just before the point where the waves are breaking and, if you have baited your hook with shellfish or bits of pork fat, you could come up with a bass or two.

Your local fishing friend may have other ideas about bait and what you may or may not catch with it. If he will take you out with him, you might have more luck.

At Póvoa de Varzim north of Oporto, the locals insist that theirs is the best beach in the country for bass. At Peniche you may also reel in bream, mullet and mackerel. At Sesimbra they say you can catch bass, shad, bream, sole, red mullet and conger eel.

Underwater spearfishing is legal in Portugal, with a licence, and one of the best places for this is off the Peniche peninsula in the waters around the Berlenga Islands. This tiny archipelago consists of four small islands, the main one of which is a National Bird Reserve, and a collection of isolated rocks and reefs, all within eight miles of the mainland. The journey by ferry-launch takes about an hour over the choppy waters, and in the summer the one small inn is open for meals and for those who want to stay. Tanks can be filled and equipment hired in Peniche.

Other popular spots are Sesimbra, Praia do Furadouro near Ovar, Póvoa de Varzim and nearby Vila do Conde. On the south coast, Sagres, Lagos, Carvoeiro and Tavira.

It is advisable to check around beforehand to locate a source of oxygen for your tank. Suppliers of diving equipment have been rather scarce in some areas, but that situation is improving. If you ask at the nearest tourist office, they can probably tell you where to find what you need.

Diving

If your interest is scuba diving rather than underwater hunting, there are any number of places to go—again, with the caution about first finding out where you can get oxygen.

To the list above add São Martinho do Porto, south of Nazaré, and the island resort of Tróia. In the Algarve: Salema, between Lagos and Sagres, where there is great excitement at the moment about the wreck of *L'Océan*, a French warship scuttled after the Battle of Lagos in 1759, which is lying in the offshore water. Also Praia da Luz, Praia da Rocha and Armação de Pêra.

Swimming

People who would rather be in the Atlantic than on it or under it have an enormous choice of places to swim. For every beach that is marked on every map, there are probably hundreds more that are too small to mention or, in some cases, too rocky to be safe for swimmers. Be careful where you swim on the western coast, where the undertow can be dangerously strong in places. Guincho, on the Estoril coast, is notorious.

The more touristy beaches come supplied with lifeguards, restaurants and bars, umbrellas and beach-beds for hire, water-skiing and windsurfing equipment and instructors on hand. At the other end of the scale, there are isolated beaches that can be reached only by boat.

Sailing

Strangely, the Algarve—which is primarily seaside resort country—has only one good marina for yachtsmen. That is the one at Vilamoura, the vast Portuguese-owned development just west of Faro. There are plans for yacht basins at Lagos and Portimão, but at the moment only Vilamoura has all the facilities that boat-owners need.

This is not to say that people do not sail on the south coast. There is any amount of small-boat activity and sailing clubs in many of the larger Algarve towns. On the west coast Setúbal, Estoril, Cascais and Figueira da Foz all have marinas.

Golf

Of the dry-land pastimes, golf is undoubtedly the most important—for those who live here and for those who come on holiday. There are already a number of fine courses and more being planned or built.

In the north there is a nine-hole course near the Pedras Salgadas spa, at Vidago. Two within reach of Oporto, where the game was first introduced to Portugal a century or so ago: eighteen holes at Espinho and nine at Praia da Miramar. North-west of Lisbon, between Torres Vedras and Lourinhã, the Vimeiro Golf Course has nine holes that can be played as eighteen, using alternative tees. The same two-for-the-price-of-one technique is used at the Estoril Sol, while the Estoril Golf Course is a straightforward eighteen-hole, par-68 layout.

The Lisbon Sports Club has a fourteen-hole course at Belas, to which another four holes are currently being added. At Aroeira, the Lisbon Country Club course is eighteen holes and par-72.

The Tróia Golf Course (eighteen holes, par-72) was built by Robert Trent Jones and was the venue for a recent Portuguese Open—to the fury of the Algarve golf clubs, who believe that they have the best and most beautiful courses in the country.

The most famous of these is the one at Penina, created by Henry Cotton from a reclaimed rice-field. Penina has both an eighteen-hole and a nine-hole course. Palmares, just east of Lagos, is one of the prettiest on the coast (but don't eat the mushrooms that grow there) with spectacular sea-views and an eighteen-hole, par-71 layout.

There are two more at Vilamoura: the Dom Pedro (par-72) and the Vilamoura (par-73). Closer to Faro, two more major developments also have fine courses: Vale do Lobo, with a total of twenty-nine holes, and Quinta do Lago, with three lots of nine holes which can apparently be played every which way. It all sounds very complicated, but real golfers are tremendously enthusiastic about it.

Tennis
Tennis has taken off in Portugal in recent years—ever since we started getting the Wimbledon Finals on television. Now we can watch top-name professionals playing at Cascais, at Roger Taylor's Tennis Centre at Vale do Lobo and at the new Burgau Sport Centre in the Algarve. All the tourist centres have courts, as do some of the health resorts.

Squash
This has been a little slower off the mark. Maybe because the courts are so expensive to build. There are one or two in the more popular Algarve tourist centres, including Burgau; in the capital, the Lisbon Casuals have courts, and there are also some in Oporto.

Cricket
If you want to play cricket on a proper pitch, rather than on a beach, you will probably have to make your Portuguese home near Lisbon or Oporto, where the game is carried on with great gusto. There have been some half-hearted attempts to get it going in the Algarve, but so far not with much success—to the disgust of my cricket-starved husband.

Riding
The Portuguese are, of course, superb horsemen, and there is no shortage of opportunities to ride, wherever you live in this country. In the Algarve it seems quite an expensive hobby, at around £6 an hour. But visitors say it is no costlier here than it is at home.

There is an Algarve Riding Club for those who have their own horses, and most of the horsey action in the south goes on around Almansil and Penina. Competitive action, that is.

Hunting

You'll hardly believe this, but there is a genuine fox-hunt here in Portugal: Equipagem de Santo Huberto, complete with MFH, a pack of hounds, stables for thirty-five mounts, and members who meet on Thursdays and Sundays to chase some unfortunate fox all over the Ribatejo. It has been going on for more than thirty years now, and if you want more information you could write to the Master, Baron F. de Beck, at Santo Estavão, Benavente.

The hunting-on-foot season starts in October, when the local people go out with dogs after small game for the pot. The business of getting a hunting licence was always difficult but it is now almost impossible because of a newly-introduced examination with sections on both theory and practice. You must know all about the species hunted, the laws concerning hunting and hunting dogs, arms and ammunition and how they should be used. You also have to do target practice. Only those who get a 75 per cent pass mark—and who can do all this in Portuguese—will be issued with a licence. Good luck.

The question of importing your own guns into Portugal is a vexed one. The Portuguese, very sensibly, are not keen on people bringing in firearms—even legally. And if they find any illegally imported weapons, there is hell to pay. We have been told on the very best authority that there is so much red tape involved at Portuguese Customs that it is really not worth the hassle; and if you don't believe me, talk to the Portuguese Consulate and to the people who are going to move you to Portugal.

The best regions for partridge (21 October to 31 December) are, in the north of Portugal, in Trás-os-Montes, and in the south, in the Algarve. Rabbit country is around the Douro river valley, and the hunting season for these is the same as for partridge. You will find quail (15 October to 31 January) in the province of Minho and around Sesimbra, duck (15 November to 15 March) in the Algarve. Hunting for hare is now forbidden in Portugal as the species is in danger of extinction in this country. Areas where hunting for anything at any time is not permitted are marked by red-and-white tin flags stuck on posts by the side of the road.

If you don't shoot to kill, there are several clubs, such as the Vilamoura Shooting Club, where international tournaments are held every year.

Skiing

Finally, and to many people's astonishment, Portugal has winter sports facilities on the country's highest mountain peak, the Malhão da Estrêla in Beira Alta. As yet, you could not really compare it with St Moritz—but give it time. So far, there are two lifts and a good selection of year-round accommodation—hikers, climbers and campers flock here in the summer—and the scenery is absolutely out of this world. Turismo Covilhã in the Praça do Município of that town are the people to contact if you are thinking of spending a winter holiday there.

We came to Portugal with the idea that there was going to be loads of lovely time to do all the things that could never be fitted in while we were working in Canada. Leisurely pursuits like sorting out the family stamp collection, reading something more edifying than our usual diet of who-dunnits, learning some new skills, bird-watching—perhaps even playing a little golf.

So far, we have had no time to do any of these things. But one of these days . . .

APPENDICES

The Provinces and District Capitals of Portugal

Federally speaking, post-Revolution Portugal is a democratic country with an elected parliament (*Assembleia de República*) of 254 members. Head of state is the President of the Republic, also democratically elected, who serves for either one or two five-year terms and who can, under certain circumstances, dissolve a sitting parliament and force a general election.

Administratively, mainland Portugal is divided into eleven provinces within which are a total of eighteen districts, each with its capital city. These districts are made up of urban and rural councils (*concelhos*) which in turn are sub-divided into any number of townships (*municípios*) and parishes (*freguesias*).

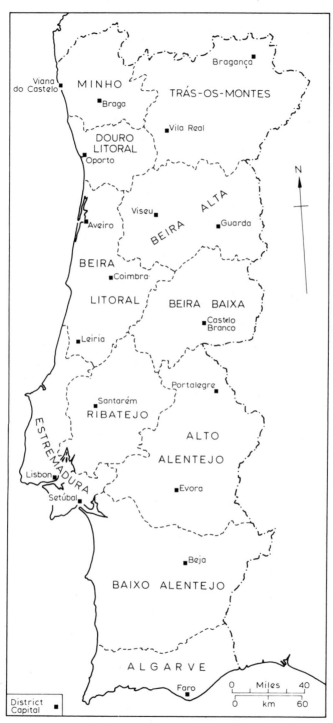

Regions and District Capitals

Portuguese Holidays

Of the twelve statutory holidays (*Feriados Obrigatórios*) observed throughout the country, two are moveable feasts: Good Friday and Corpus Christi, which is usually in June. Those that do not move are:

1 January, fortunately. All Portugal celebrates enthusiastically on New Year's Eve, and *Ano Novo* is devoted to recovering from hangovers and lack of sleep due to the noise of hooters, motor-bikes, fireworks, shouting, singing and the banging of saucepan and dustbin lids.

25 April, *O Dia da Liberdade*, is a political occasion commemorating the 1974 Revolution and the end of more than thirty years of dictatorship. In Lisbon and the other cities, this is a day of parades, rallies, speeches and general jollification.

1 May, Labour Day (*Dia do Trabalho*), is celebrated in Portugal as it is in most other European countries.

10 June is Portugal's national day, *Dia de Portugal*, when the country honours its most famous poet, Luís de Camões, who wrote the epic "*Os Lusíadas*" in praise of the Portuguese people.

15 August, the Feast of the Assumption (*Assunção de Nossa Senhora*), is more strictly observed in Lisbon and the north than it is in the Algarve, where everything closes and most people go to the beach.

5 October, *Dia da República*, commemorates the founding in 1910 of the first Republican Government of Portugal, following the death of Dom Carlos and the departure of his heir, Dom Manuel II, for exile in Britain.

1 November, All Saints' Day (*Festa de Todos-os-Santos*), is not only a religious occasion but a day of special significance in Portugal. In 1755 thousands of people, including most of those

attending All Saints' Day services, lost their lives in the great Lisbon earthquake and the tidal wave that followed. The fact that almost all those who were languishing in the Lisbon prisons and low haunts escaped has puzzled ecclesiastics ever since.

1 December, *Dia de Restauração*, is the anniversary of the restoration of the Portuguese Crown in 1640 after sixty years of Spanish rule.

8 December, the Feast of the Immaculate Conception, is a bank holiday, and so, of course, is . . .

25 December, *Natal*, which is very much a family holiday in Portugal.

Christmas Eve, though not an official holiday, is the one day in the year when Portugal's casinos shut up shop, so the staff can enjoy Christmas dinner with their families. A great many Portuguese restaurants also close for the same reason, but most will be open again on Christmas Day. Boxing Day and Easter Monday are not holidays in Portugal, and if one of the *Feriados Obrigatórios* falls on a Saturday or Sunday, that is everyone's bad luck. Here, the holiday is not moved forward to the following Monday.

On a *Feriado Obrigatório* the banks, post offices, offices and shops are all closed in the towns; pubs and restaurants usually stay open. In a small village, particularly one that caters for tourists, you may well find a grocery shop that is open for business—though the bread will be yesterday's, since the bakers are on holiday.

Fairs, Festivals and Pilgrimages

It is not possible to list all the special Portuguese occasions that are celebrated all over the country. These are just a few of the major ones.

January

Oporto — *Festa de São Conçalo e São Cristovão.*

Aveiro — *Festa de São Sebastião* at the end of the month.

February

The pre-Lenten Carnival is celebrated all over Portugal and with particular vigour in Lisbon, Loulé, Ovar, Nazaré, Mourão and Oporto.

March—or **April**, depending on the date of Easter.

Holy Week celebrations in many major centres, including Braga, Póvoa de Varzim and Ovar.

Loulé — Festival of *Nossa Senhora de Piedade*, two weeks after Easter.

Lisbon — *Procissão do Senhor dos Passos da Graça.*

April

Santarém — The two-week Milagre Fair, starting on the second Sunday.

Braga — Whitsun Pilgrimage, six weeks after Easter.

Barcelos — *Romaria do Senhor Bom Jesús de Fão* at the end of April.

May

Guimarães — *Festa das Cruzes* in early May.

Sesimbra	*Festa do Senhor das Chagas*, fishermen's festival.
Barcelos	*Festa das Cruzes.*
Viana do Castelo	*Festa da Senhora das Rosas* (mid-May).
Fátima	Night of 12th–13th: Pilgrimage to the Shrine. These pilgrimages are held through the summer on the same night of each month through to October.
Coimbra	*Queima das Fitas*, end of academic year celebrations in mid-May.
Santarém	Two-week Ribatejo Fair, starting the fourth Sunday of May.
June	The month of the Popular Saints (Anthony on the 12th and 13th, John on the 23rd and 24th, Peter on the 28th and 29th) who are celebrated in towns and villages all over Portugal.
Moncão	*Festa do Corpo de Deus*, Corpus Christi pageant.
Amarante	*Festa de São Conçalo*, a combination religious festival and fertility celebration on the first Saturday in June.
Matosinhos	*Festas do Senhor de Matosinhos*, with fireworks and bull-running.
Braga Caldas da Rainha Vila do Conde	Midsummer celebrations on the 23rd, 24th and 25th, with the Holy Bath at Caldas da Rainha.
July Vila Franca de Xira	*Festa da Colete Encardo* on the first and second Sundays—bull-running.
Tomar	*Festa dos Tabuleiros*, folk festival on alternate years.
Santo Tirso	São Bento Pilgrimage and Fair (10th and 11th).
Guimarães	*Romaria* at nearby São Torcato.
Aveiro	*Festa da Ria* (seaweed fishers' regatta) and the International Folk Festival.

Estoril	Sea Festival and *Feira de Artesanato* (crafts festival).
Setúbal	*Feira de Santiago* (regional agricultural and craft show).
Cascais	*Festa de Cascais*, from middle to end of the month.
Mirandela	*Festas do Senhor do Amparo e Feria de Santiago*.

August

Praia da Rocha	Carnival, from 1st to 3rd of the month.
Peniche	*Festas da Senhora da Boa Viagem*, boat processions.
Peneda-Gerês	*Festas do São Pedro* with processions and bullfights.
Guimarães	*Festas Gualterianas* on the 5th, and *Festas de Vizela*.
Batalha	*Festas da Senhora da Vitória*.
Beja	*Feira de São Lourenço e Santa Maria*: fair and bullfights.
Viana do Castelo	At the weekend nearest 20 August: *Romaria de Nossa Senhora da Agonia*, a three-day festival, fair, processions, etc.
Mirando do Douro	*Festa de Santa Bárbara* on the third Sunday.
Caminha	*Festas de Santa Rita de Cássia*: processions with traditional costumes.
Braga	*Festa da Senhora da Saúde e Soedade*, mid-month fishermen's festival.
Alcobaça	*Feira de São Bernardo*, agricultural show.
Vila Viçosa	Mid-August horse fair.
Santarém	Minor fairs all through the month.

September

Lamego	Pilgrimage on the 8th.
Nazaré	*Romaria* (8th–10th) with processions, dancing, bullfights.

Ponte de Lima	New Fairs with dancing, fireworks etc. on second and third weekends.
Miranda do Douro	*Romaria Nossa Senhora do Nazo* (7th and 8th).
Praia da Torreira	*Romaria de São Paio de Torreira*: festival, boat blessing and traditional Holy Bath.
Beja	*Romaria da Senhor de Aires*: church festival and bullfights.
Buçaco	*Festa da Senhora da Vitória em Comemoração da Batalha do Buçaco* (Wellington's victory against the French at Buçaco in 1810).
Elvas	*Festa do Senhor Jesús da Piedade.* Also *Feira de São Mateus.*
Póvoa de Varzim	*Festas da Senhora das Dores*, religious festival.
Palmela	*Festa das Vindimas*, the vintage festival.

October

Vila Franca de Xira	*Festas Bravas* and Annual Fair on the first Sunday of the month.
Santarém	Two-week Piedade Fair starting the second Sunday.
Chaves	*Feira dos Santos.*
Faro	*Feira de Santa Iria.*
Moura	*Festa da Senhora do Monte do Carmo*, processions.
Fátima	*Última Peregrinação Anual*, the last pilgrimage of the year to the Shrine.

November

Penafiel	*Feira de São Martinho.*

Schooling in Portugal

With one exception, the families we know here with school-age children send their offspring either to one of the several international schools in Portugal or else back to a British boarding school. They all moan about the cost.

The exception is an Irish couple who are putting their youngsters through the Portuguese school system at a fraction of the cost of having them educated in Britain or Eire—never mind the expense of flying them out to Portugal for holidays. It took a while for the children to get used to being the only *estrangeiros* in class. But once that hurdle was cleared, they settled down happily and are doing extremely well. And their parents are more than satisfied with the results.

You cannot, apparently, simply take your child and enrol it in the local school. Permission must be obtained through that local school from the Ministry of Education in Lisbon (Av. 4 de Outubro 107) before a foreign student can be accepted into the Portuguese school system. If he or she has had previous schooling, the Ministry wants to examine all the pertinent papers before giving that permission.

Take every relevant bit of paper you can lay your hands on, our friends advise, to prove how long your child has been at school outside Portugal and what scholastic level was reached. Also take a handful of official paper, because there is a great deal of official writing involved. But they also say that it is not nearly so complicated as it sounds and they were most agreeably surprised at the ease and friendliness of the whole procedure.

Schooling is, naturally, in Portuguese. But English and French are also on the curriculum. There is one point that should be mentioned: if you are thinking of going this route, you will be asked if your child speaks any Portuguese. Make sure that he or she does, if only a little. And arrange, before term starts, for a few private lessons so that the child is not completely at sea.

Though it is improving, the standard of Portuguese education is not yet as high as it is in some other European countries, and therefore parents who come to live here do have to give the matter of schooling some serious thought.

Fortunately there are quite a few options, certainly in the Algarve and in the area around Lisbon. There it is possible to give a child a good private education up to A Levels. The fees, so we are constantly being told, are steep—but so they are in Britain.

In the south of Portugal, the Algarve International School at Porches near Lagôa takes children of all nationalities (including Portuguese) from kindergarten up to O Level—about four hundred of them. It is essentially a day school, with its own bus service to collect pupils from the surrounding area, but a small number of weekly boarders are accepted and cared for by resident house-parents. The school is the centre in southern Portugal for the London University GCE examinations.

Prince Henry International College at Vale do Lobo, Almansil gives all instruction in English. It calls itself a day/boarding school and accepts children from three years old in the kindergarten. Tuition in the senior school (twelve to sixteen years) is directed towards the General Certificate of Education of Cambridge University.

The Barlavento English School at Espiche, 8600 Lagos, is a small privately run establishment for small children of all nationalities.

In Lisbon, the American International School has been going for some thirty years, a non-denominational, co-educational school offering an American curriculum to students who range from kindergarten age to seventeen years. The address, if you would like a prospectus, is Apartado 10, Carnaxide, 2795 Linda-a-Velha.

About ten miles out of Lisbon, St Julian's School is the largest and probably the best known in the area. A co-educational day school founded more than fifty years ago for British children, it now has more than 750 children of all nationalities—half of them Portuguese. St Julian's is divided into three sections. In the First School (3½ to seven years) teaching is in English, by British-trained staff. The East Wing (seven to eighteen years), also in English, offers Public Schools Common Entrance, O and A Level Cambridge Board and the CSE (SREB). The North Wing is the Portuguese section, where the official Portuguese programmes are taught and exams taken. You can get more information from the Headmaster at Quinta Nova, Carcavelos, 2775 Parede.

St Anthony's International Primary School (Avenida de Portugal 11, 2765 Estoril) provides a primary education in English for children up to twelve years of age. Portuguese is taught, as it is in all foreign schools here, and they are thoroughly up to date, with things like audio-visual teaching aids and computer studies for the seniors.

St George's School (Vila Conçalves, Quinta das Loureiras, Estrada Nacional, 2750 Cascais) is an English day-school catering for children from four to thirteen years. Pupils are prepared for Common Entrance and British public schools scholarships, and there is a similar programme for American students.

St Dominic's College (Rua Outeiro da Polima, 2780 Arneiro) is the only Catholic school for English-speaking children in Portugal, though children of other religions and nationalities are welcomed. The original college was founded more than a century ago in Belém, but the relatively new premises near Sassoeiras have all the most modern facilities. The age range is from four to sixteen, and children are prepared for O Levels.

There are also some excellent facilities for small children.

In Sintra, the Casa dos Santos Infant School teaches children from three to six of all nationalities, and even smaller ones (one to three years) on an hourly basis. All in English. For more information write to the school at Quinta do Relógio, 2710 Sintra.

Nursery Class has been in business for more than twenty years at Rua da Arriaga 39, 1200 Lisboa. From 9 a.m. to 12.30

every weekday morning, English is taught to children from three to six years old.

O Pincho Kindergarten at Quinta de S. João, Rebelva, Carcavelos, is less specific about what it actually teaches. But it has been going for several years and will accept children from two to six years old.

Tax-paying Calendar

January	*Imposto Profissional.*
	Half of *Contribuição Predial.*
May	*Imposto Sobre Veículos.*
June	*Imposto Complementar* to be filed.
July	*Imposto Complementar* to be filed, if not already done in June.
	Other half of *Contribuição Predial.*
October	*Imposto Complementar* to be paid.
December	* Thirteenth Month payment to employees.

* This is not, obviously, a tax—but it is something that should not be forgotten.

How to Write a Portuguese Cheque

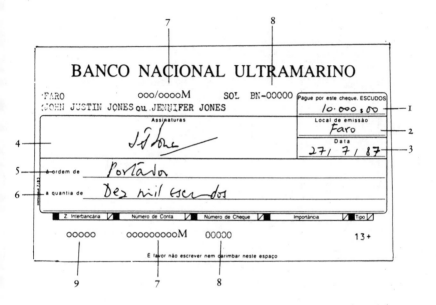

1 Amount in figures, using continental fullstop instead of British comma to indicate thousands.
2 The town where this cheque is being written.
3 The date, written the British (not American) way.*
4 Your signature.
5 Payee's name—in this case, Bearer.
6 Amount, which can often be written out in English.
7 Your account number.
8 The number of this cheque.
9 The bank's branch identification.

* Get accustomed to crossing the figure 7, as all continentals do.

How to Fill in a Portuguese Deposit Slip

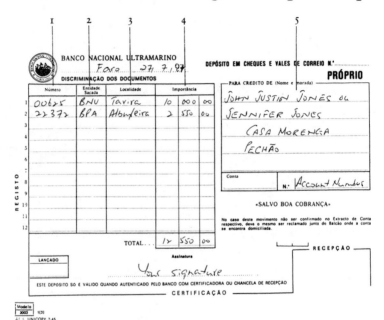

1. The number of the cheque deposited (see previous page).
2. The initials of the bank from which that cheque was issued; in this case, Banco Nacional Ultramarino and Banco Português do Atlantico.
3. Where that bank is located.
4. The amount of the cheque deposited.
5. The name in which your account is held, and your address.

Useful Addresses in Lisbon

Airport Information   Telephone 889181
Automobile Club (Automóvel Clube de Portugal)
    Rua de Rosa Araújo 24–26
British Community Council
    Rua S. Sebastião Pedreira 122–3°
British Historical Society of Portugal
    Colégio dos Inglesinhos, Rua da São Boaventura 5
British Hospital
    Rua Saraiva de Carvalho 49
British Institute (Instituto Britânica em Portugal)
    Rua de Luís Fernandes 3
British-Portuguese Chamber of Commerce
    Rua da Estrêla 8
Corpo Santo Church (Irish Dominican Fathers)
    Largo do Corpo Santo
Lisbon Tourist Office
    Palacio Foz, Praça dos Restauradores
St David's Society of Portugal
    Rua Alto do Duque 49, Restelo
St George's Church (Church of England)
    Rua S. Jorge (Chaplain—Rua da Estrêla 4)

Useful Addresses in Oporto

American Library
    Rua da Firmeza 521
British Association
    Rua Infante D. Henriques 8
British Council
    Rua do Breyner 115
British Hospital
    Rua da Bandeirinha 12
Oporto Cricket and Lawn Tennis Club
    Rua Campo Alegre 536
Oporto Golf Club
    Pedreira, Silvalde, Espinho
St James's Anglican Church
    Largo da Maternidade, Julio Dinis
São António Hospital
    Rua José de Carvalho
Stella Maris (International Seamen's Club)
    Rua da Fresca 78, Leça Leixões

Portuguese Consulates in Great Britain

Consulate General, Silver City House, 62 Brompton Road,
   London SW3 1BJ
   Telephone 01-581 8722/3/4
4 Knoll Court, Sneyd Park, Bristol BS9 1QX
   Telephone 0272-685042
Gogar Park, Glasgow Road, Edinburgh EH12 9DJ
   Telephone 031-339 5345
14 Mount Street, Manchester M2 3NN
   Telephone 061-834 1821/2
8 York Street, St Helier, Jersey, Channel Islands
   Telephone 0534-77188

British Embassy in Lisbon
Rua S. Domingos à Lapa 35-37
   Telephone 661191

British Consulates in Portugal
Oporto: Av. de Boavista 3072
   Telephone 684789
Figueira da Foz: Quinta de Santa Margarida, Estrada de
Tavorede
   Telephone 22235
Portimão: Rua Santa Isabel 21
   Telephone 23071

Index